Lecture Notes in Computer Science 15267

Founding Editors

Gerhard Goos
Juris Hartmanis

The series Lecture Notes in Computer Science (LNCS), including its subseries Lecture Notes in Artificial Intelligence (LNAI) and Lecture Notes in Bioinformatics (LNBI), has established itself as a medium for the publication of new developments in computer science and information technology research, teaching, and education.

LNCS enjoys close cooperation with the computer science R & D community, the series counts many renowned academics among its volume editors and paper authors, and collaborates with prestigious societies. Its mission is to serve this international community by providing an invaluable service, mainly focused on the publication of conference and workshop proceedings and postproceedings. LNCS commenced publication in 1973.

Claudia Blaas-Schenner ·
Christoph Niethammer · Tobias Haas
Editors

Recent Advances in the Message Passing Interface

31st European MPI Users' Group Meeting, EuroMPI 2024
Perth, WA, Australia, September 25–27, 2024
Proceedings

 Springer

Editors
Claudia Blaas-Schenner
VSC Research Center, TU Wien
Operngasse, Wien, Austria

Christoph Niethammer
HLRS, University of Stuttgart
Stuttgart, Baden-Württemberg, Germany

Tobias Haas
HLRS, University of Stuttgart
Stuttgart, Baden-Württemberg, Germany

ISSN 0302-9743   ISSN 1611-3349 (electronic)
Lecture Notes in Computer Science
ISBN 978-3-031-73369-7   ISBN 978-3-031-73370-3 (eBook)
https://doi.org/10.1007/978-3-031-73370-3

This Springer imprint is published by the registered company Springer Nature Switzerland AG
The registered company address is: Gewerbestrasse 11, 6330 Cham, Switzerland

If disposing of this product, please recycle the paper.

Preface

The Message Passing Interface (MPI) is the *de facto* standard for parallel programming, especially for inter-node communication. It is standardized by the MPI Forum, which released the first version of the MPI standard three decades ago (MPI-1.0, 5 May 1994). Through the diligent work of the MPI Forum the MPI standard has evolved over the years to version MPI-4.1, which was released on 2 November 2023. Multiple implementations are available and used on compute clusters and supercomputers throughout the world.

The annual EuroMPI conference is the preeminent meeting for users, developers, and researchers to interact and discuss new developments and applications of MPI. This includes new proposed concepts and extensions to the MPI standard, libraries and languages built on top of MPI, interfaces to other standards in parallel programming, applications and optimizations to new architectures and networks, novel algorithms, and tools, with particular focus on quality, portability, performance, and scalability. The EuroMPI meeting has a long, rich tradition, and has been held annually since 1994.

In its 31st edition, EuroMPI continued to focus on advancing the ubiquitous MPI model and specification of parallel programming. It encompassed extensions and alternative interfaces for high-performance heterogeneous and hybrid systems, benchmarks, tools, parallel I/O, fault tolerance, and parallel applications using MPI and other interfaces. Through the presentation of contributed papers, posters, and invited talks, the conference presented a complete overview of MPI, its current usage in the parallel programming landscape, and its future directions. The conference provided ample opportunities for attendees to interact and share ideas and experiences to contribute to the improvement and furthering of message-passing and related parallel programming paradigms.

EuroMPI/Australia 2024 was hosted by the Pawsey Supercomputing Research Centre in Perth, Australia, from 25–27 September 2024, and co-located with the OpenMP Language Committee face-to-face meeting (16–20 September 2024), MPI Forum meeting (23–24 September 2024), and IWOMP 2024 – 20th International Workshop on OpenMP (23–25 September 2024). Having these meetings grouped together allowed attendees to interact and share ideas and experiences to contribute to the improvement and advancement of message-passing, shared-memory parallelism, and related parallel programming paradigms – and their combined usage.

The joint IWOMP and EuroMPI/Australia 2024 keynote was given by Sarah Pearce, Director of the Low Telescope of the Square Kilometer Array Observatory, on "Building a time machine. How supercomputing is giving astronomy a new window into the past" – it is not included in the proceedings.

EuroMPI/Australia 2024 invited high-quality, full-paper submissions on all topics related to message-passing parallel programming with MPI and related or competing models. Papers were reviewed for quality, originality, clarity, correctness, technical strength, and relevance to the topics of the meeting. EuroMPI/Australia 2024 received 19 full-paper submissions. Each full-paper submission got at least three reviews (most submissions got four reviews) from members of the program committee. A conflict-of-interest declaration was used for contributions co-authored by any committee members, i.e., affected committee members could not review their own contributions, were not able to see the names of the reviewers, and could not see the reviewer discussion about the affected papers. Reviews were single blind, i.e., reviewers could see the names of the authors but not the other way around. If necessary, there was a discussion period for the program committee to come to a clear consensus about a submission, but there was no rebuttal mechanism. Out of the 19 full-paper submissions, 8 papers were accepted for presentation at the conference and inclusion in the proceedings with the final decision made by the program committee chairs based on the reviews and discussions.

Poster and short-paper submissions were also possible. These received two single-blind reviews each and are not included in the proceedings.

The contributions spanned a wide field of topics and so do the ones included in these proceedings. We start with the contribution that won the best paper award, which presented a new intermediate representation (IR) for compilers that eases the correctness checking of parallel applications. This shows the importance of tools and the interaction with other parallel programming models for MPI today. It is followed by another contribution around the topic of IR that focused on improving the compiler's understanding of MPI for optimization purposes. Concerning performance, general purpose GPUs (GPGPUs) play an essential role in high-performance computing today and thus it was no surprise to see two papers focusing on the analysis of current limitations and potential API extensions for GPGPUs in MPI. But also more classical topics about algorithmic and memory subsystem-related improvements for MPI libraries were covered. Finally, two contributions around the ecosystem of MPI were included. Here the application of the relatively new MPI sessions mechanism for dynamic in situ tasks as well as a new test harness for the increasingly important MPI correctness tools were presented.

The complete information and program for EuroMPI/Australia 2024 can be found on the webpage https://events.vsc.ac.at/e/EuroMPI2024.

September 2024   Claudia Blaas-Schenner
                                                Christoph Niethammer
                                                        Tobias Haas

Organization

General Chairs

Claudia Blaas-Schenner	TU Wien, Austria
Christoph Niethammer	University of Stuttgart, Germany

Program Committee Chairs

Claudia Blaas-Schenner	TU Wien, Austria
Christoph Niethammer	University of Stuttgart, Germany
Tobias Haas	University of Stuttgart, Germany

Publication Chair

Tobias Haas	University of Stuttgart, Germany

Publicity and Web Chairs

Julia Wimmer	TU Wien, Austria
Claudia Blaas-Schenner	TU Wien, Austria

Finance Chair

Brian Smith	Cornelis Networks, USA

Local Chairs

Alexis Espinosa	Pawsey Supercomputing Research Centre, Australia
Emily Kahal	Pawsey Supercomputing Research Centre, Australia

Registration Chair

Karina Nuñez   Pawsey Supercomputing Research Centre,
                                Australia

Steering Committee

Jack Dongarra   University of Tennessee Knoxville, USA
William Gropp   University of Illinois at Urbana-Champaign, USA
Jesper Larsson Träff   TU Wien, Austria
Pavan Balaji   Meta, USA

Program Committee

Julien Adam   ParaTools SAS, France
Purushotham Bangalore   University of Alabama, USA
Wes Bland   Meta, USA
Aurélien Bouteiller   University of Tennessee Knoxville, USA
Jim Dinan   NVIDIA, USA
Matthew Dosanjh   Sandia National Laboratories, USA
Pascal Jahan Elahi   Pawsey Supercomputing Research Centre,
                                Australia
Ryan E. Grant   Queen's University, Canada
William Gropp   University of Illinois at Urbana-Champaign, USA
Jeff Hammond   NVIDIA, Finland
Marc-André Hermanns   RWTH Aachen University, Germany
Julien Jaeger   CEA, France
Stefano Markidis   KTH Royal Institute of Technology, Sweden
Guillaume Mercier   Inria, France
Konstantinos Parasyris   Lawrence Livermore National Laboratory, USA
Howard Pritchard   Los Alamos National Laboratory, USA
Kento Sato   RIKEN R-CCS, Japan
Martin Schreiber   Université Grenoble Alpes, France
Joseph Schuchart   Stony Brook University, USA
Martin Schulz   Technical University of Munich, Germany
David E. Singh   Universidad Carlos III de Madrid, Spain
Jeff Squyres   Cisco, USA
Hari Subramoni   Ohio State University, USA
Shinji Sumimoto   University of Tokyo, Japan

Rajeev Thakur   Argonne National Laboratory, USA
Jesper Larsson Träff   TU Wien, Austria

Additional Reviewers

Kaushik Kandadi Suresh
Goutham Kalikrishna Reddy Kuncham
Benjamin Michalowicz
Akshay Paniraja Guptha
Noah Pavuk
Ken Raffenetti
Bharath Ramesh
Shulei Xu
Hui Zhou

Sponsors

Pawsey Supercomputing Research Centre, Australia

MPI Forum, https://www.mpi-forum.org

Contents

Compile-Time Correctness Checks
and Optimization

SPMD IR: Unifying SPMD and Multi-value IR Showcased for Static Verification of Collectives

Semih Burak[1]([✉])([iD]), Ivan R. Ivanov[2]([iD]), Jens Domke[2]([iD]),
and Matthias Müller[1]([iD])

[1] Chair for High Performance Computing, IT Center, RWTH Aachen University,
Aachen, Germany
burak@itc.rwth-aachen.de
[2] RIKEN Center for Computational Science, Kobe, Japan

Abstract. To effectively utilize modern HPC clusters, inter-node communication and related single program, multiple data (SPMD) parallel programming models such as MPI are inevitable. Current tools and compilers that employ analyses of SPMD models often have the limitation of only supporting one model or implementing the necessary abstraction internally. This makes the analysis and effort for the abstraction neither reusable nor the tool extensible to other models without extensive changes to the tool itself.

This work proposes an SPMD IR as part of a multi-layer program representation and accompanying compiler passes to explicitly express the results of abstraction and multi-value analysis. The SPMD IR makes the executing processes of operations explicit and differentiates between static and dynamic cases. It is implemented as a prototype in the MLIR LLVM infrastructure and is comprised of the SPMD dialect and two compiler passes, supporting MPI, SHMEM, and NCCL, including hybrid cases.

To evaluate the proposed IR, verification of collective communication was chosen as a use case. For that, this work reimplements and extends PARCOACH's static approach on the SPMD IR and assesses it by an expanded micro-benchmark suite in MPI, SHMEM, and NCCL. Achieving similar detection accuracy, the evaluation shows that the SPMD IR's level of abstraction is strong enough for PARCOACH's analyses and generic enough for increased extensibility. The prototype also constitutes the first collectives verification of SHMEM, NCCL, and their combinations (with MPI).

Keywords: Parallel IR · MLIR · Static Analysis · Correctness · MPI · SHMEM · NCCL

1 Introduction

HPC systems are not only becoming increasingly heterogeneous in terms of hardware, the software necessary to effectively utilize this hardware is also getting

C. Blaas-Schenner et al. (Eds.): EuroMPI 2024, LNCS 15267, pp. 3–20, 2025.
https://doi.org/10.1007/978-3-031-73370-3_1

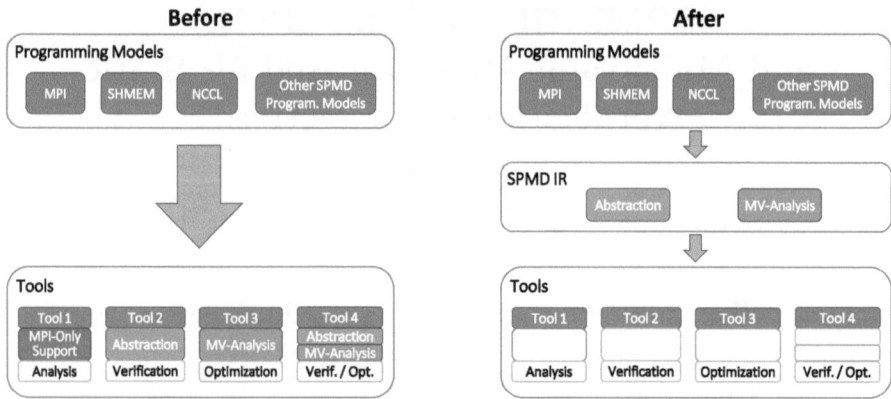

Fig. 1. Illustrates how tools would work on parallel programming models before and after the introduction of a unifying SPMD IR.

increasingly complex. One part of this heterogeneous architecture is the multi-node composition that necessitates inter-node communication, making single program, multiple data (SPMD) parallel programming models such as MPI [10] inevitable.

While MPI is the de facto standard for distributed-memory systems, other models that combine SPMD or inter-node communication aspects with other programming paradigms are getting more frequent too. For example, (OPEN)SHMEM [18] is mainly a partitioned global address space (PGAS) programming model with a particular focus on one-sided communication. However, it also includes collective communication and can be used for implementing SPMD-like programs. NCCL [13], on the other hand, provides inter-GPU communication primitives in the form of collective and point-to-point communication and involves GPU-specific elements, e.g., stream semantics. They can also be combined to make use of each programming model's advantages and features.

With even more programming models and combinations available, current tools, e.g., for correctness verification or performance optimization, often have the limitation of only supporting one or implementing the necessary abstraction internally. A similar problem exists for the multi-value (MV) analysis, a crucial part of many static tools [1,5,29] for SPMD programs; the implementation and result of the analysis are not reusable across tools. Figure 1 illustrates on the left how some tools only support MPI (cf. Tool 1), while other tools duplicate the MV-Analysis and necessary effort for the abstraction (cf. Tool 2–4). Those components are not reusable, and the tools are only extensible to other models with extensive changes to the tool itself.

One of those tools for SPMD programs is PARCOACH [20]. It is originally a tool that verifies collective communication of MPI programs based on a static and an optional subsequent dynamic approach. Although it was later extended to other programming models such as OPENMP [17], PARCOACH's latest release versions [6] indicate that the tool is mainly maintained and developed for MPI.

To solve the aforementioned problems and thereby provide increased extensibility and reusability of static tools for SPMD-like programming models, this work proposes an SPMD IR as part of a multi-layer program representation. It is implemented as a prototype in the MLIR [8] LLVM infrastructure and is comprised of the SPMD dialect and two compiler passes. The first compiler pass unifies the API function calls of possibly multiple different programming models and generates SPMD IR operations and operands instead. The second pass then analyses this unified abstract IR and performs an extended multi-value analysis to derive properties of values and operations important for analyzing SPMD programs.

Since the SPMD dialect can be used alongside and in combination with other dialects in MLIR, the general expressiveness of the total IR is not diminished. The SPMD IR tries to find a good trade-off between the abstraction level and the transformation's feasibility. Adding support for a new programming model would only necessitate altering the transformation pass to the unifying SPMD IR. Figure 1 shows on the right how the SPMD IR enables tools to reuse the effort for abstraction and the MV-Analysis. It helps to abstract the problem and solution.

This paper makes the following contributions:

- Designing a unifying SPMD IR that can represent core functionality of SPMD programming models and the notion of multi-values and make statically useful SPMD properties explicit for distributed-memory, PGAS, and GPU programs (Sect. 3.1, Sect. 3.2).
- Implementing a prototype of the proposed IR as a dialect and necessary analyses and transformations as compiler passes in MLIR, incl. those for MPI (Sect. 3.3).
- Providing a port of PARCOACH's static approach on collectives verification for MPI to the SPMD IR and showcasing an evaluation of the proof-of-concept compared to PARCOACH, with two extensions for static cases (Sect. 4.1, Sect. 4.3).
- Extending the micro-benchmark suite for collectives verification [5], providing ports to SHMEM and NCCL, and adding hybrid test cases (Sect. 4.2).

2   Background to MLIR

The purpose of intermediate representations (IRs) in compilers is generally to facilitate optimizations before lowering to low-level or even machine code. Compared to other existing IRs like LLVM IR [7], MLIR [8] is more extensible and supports mixing high-level and low-level abstractions and encapsulating domain-specific semantics by means of so-called *dialects*. That is why this work chooses MLIR to implement the SPMD IR so that SPMD-related information can be expressed next to other high-level parallelism representations, e.g., shared-memory or device parallelism and other high-level program structures such as loops. This may allow even stronger optimizations and analyses.

A dialect is a collection of custom operations, types, and attributes. As each dialect can seamlessly interact with other dialects, MLIR provides a toolset to

```
1   func.func @multPosByX(%arg_ref: memref<?xf64>, %arg_size: index,
                          %arg_c_x: f64) -> () {
2     %c0_index = arith.constant() {value = 0 : index} () -> index
3     ... // define other constants
4     scf.for %idx = %c0_index to %arg_size step %c1_index
               : (index, index, index, i32) -> () {
5        %value = memref.load(%arg_ref, %idx) : (memref<?xf64>, index) -> f64
6        %cmpRes = arith.cmpf (%value, %c0_f64) {..olt..} : (f64, f64) -> i1
7        scf.if(%cmpRes) : (i1) -> () {
8           %newValue = arith.mulf(%value, %arg_c_x) : (f64, f64) -> f64
9           memref.store(%newValue, %arg_ref, %idx):(f64,memref<?xf64>,index)->()
10       }
11    }
12  }
13
14  func.func @main(...) -> i32   {
15     ... // define constants and other omitted operations
16     %ref = memref.alloca(%size) : (index) -> memref<?xf64>
17     ... // fill "array" (ref) with values
18  func.call @multPosByX(%ref, %size, %c_x) : (memref<?xf64>, index, f64) -> ()
19     ...
20  }
```

Fig. 2. An example C program represented in MLIR, which multiplies x to each positive element of an array. Red highlights the dialects, orange the values, and blue the types.

develop an expressive IR composed of multiple levels and semantics. The basic IR constructs are operations, attributes, regions, blocks, values, and types. An MLIR program representation consists of a sequence of operations, and an operation can have multiple results, operands, attributes, and regions. Results and operands are static single assignment (SSA) values, i.e., assigned exactly once, and tailored to represent dynamic information, as opposed to attributes, which are designed for static information. Each value and attribute must have a defined type.

Operations can have regions attached to them, which contain blocks that are lists of operations, allowing a nested IR construction with structure. The control-flow semantics within and among regions are to be defined by the respective operation. For example, the if operation of the scf dialect has two regions, from which only one will be executed depending on its bool-like operand.

An example of a C program lowered to MLIR is shown in Fig. 2. This program multiplies each positive element of an array by a constant x. In Line 16, a memory reference of dynamic size is created, named ref. It allows loading, modifying, or storing the values at the respective memory location, similar to a pointer or an array in C. These operations are grouped in the memref dialect. In Line 18, multPosByX is called with the memory reference, allocated size, and constant x as arguments. While Line 5 loads the array value, Lines 8 and 9 compute the new value and store it back into the array.

For instance, this IR uses the arith dialect for arithmetic and representing constants and the scf dialect for representing control-flow semantics such as branching or loops. An example of an attribute is given in Line 2, where the value of the arithmetic constant is statically defined as zero. Line 4 demonstrates the usage of the for operation in the scf dialect. It contains a single region and block that has a defined number of executions based on its lower bound, upper bound, and step operands. It further defines an induction variable as an argument to its region for the loop index. Here, the loop is executed once for each element stored at the memory reference `arg_ref`.

Although the upstream MLIR project provides built-in types, attributes, and dialects, there is no standard prescribing which set of dialects should be used; dialects can be mixed and matched for the purpose at hand. A developer can either extend existing dialects or define their own one and thereby make use of the common and rich MLIR infrastructure for their domain problem.

Polygeist [11] is a tool consisting of multiple compiler passes that can transform C/C++ to MLIR and can convert one MLIR representation to another MLIR representation for optimization purposes. However, in the set of dialects Polygeist emits and also in the currently available MLIR dialects, the semantics of an SPMD program and the notion of multi-values can only be represented in the context of loops in the form of loop-invariant values. SSA values appear as they represent and contain the same data for each process.

Furthermore, MLIR has no concept of executing the same program by multiple processes. There is no indication which process is executing which part of the program at the level of MLIR. Specifically, the library calls of programming models such MPI or NCCL are represented by external function calls, and the only information given besides the function name are the input and output value types.

3   Unifying SPMD and Multi-value IR

This section first presents an extension for a multi-value analysis in MLIR and then the SPMD IR design and implementation based on a complete workflow.

3.1   Multi-value IR

Generally, a variable or value is called *multi-value* (MV) if its runtime-value may differ for a subset of processes and is called single-value (SV) otherwise [1]. An *MV-seed* operation is a special operation that produces MVs by definition (e.g., operations getting process IDs, analogous to `MPI_Comm_rank`). Starting from that, new MVs can be yielded through operations using these values or when the control flow diverges through a conditional depending on an MV.

Tiotto et al. [25] implemented an extensible multi-value analysis, which they call uniformity-analysis, for GPU programs in MLIR. They use it in their SYCL-MLIR compiler for a loop internalization optimization to determine whether a loop is executed in a divergent region. Among others, it builds upon a reaching-definition and alias analysis.

This work adapts their approach to SPMD programs, adds an execution kind and executing process analysis, and expresses the results of this *extended multi-value* analysis as attributes in the IR. Table 1 shows the attributes introduced by the SPMD IR, from which three are relevant for the MV notion: `isMultiValued`, `executionKind`, and `executed(Not)By`. `isMultiValued` is used to declare a conditional as depending on a multi-value and thereby being divergent for the processes executing it. This information is crucial for the evaluation based on the collectives verification in Sect. 4.

Table 1. Set of the SPMD IR attributes.

Attribute	Values
isBlocking	True, False
isBuffered	True, False
usedModel	32-bit integer, starting from 0
isMultiValued	True, False
executionKind	All, AllBut, Static, Dynamic, One, AllButOne
executed(Not)By	List of process IDs (not) executing the operation

The attribute `executionKind` further specifies for each operation whether it is executed by all processes with value `All` (often implicit default behavior in an SPMD program), a *known* subset of processes with `Static` (specifically useful for hardware-specific code generating tools such as the PPL [22]), an *unknown* (sub)set of processes with `Dynamic`, and a possibly *unknown single* process with `One` (potentially useful for representing tasking). Further, the value `AllBut` covers the case of having only static information on the processes not executing an operation. The value `AllButOne` is the counterpart to value `One`. For both execution kinds `Static` and `AllBut`, it is also analyzed and denoted which processes are (not) executing a certain operation by the attribute `isExecuted(Not)By`.

For the specification of `executionKind`, the prototype assumes an execution by `All` processes and analyze multi-valued conditionals in the program. For example, when the condition of a branch operation is of form (`rank == 0 || ...`), then the operations nested in the `then` branch have a `Static executionKind` with the executing process IDs specified. The operations in the `else` branch would then be of kind `AllBut` with the process IDs not executing them specified. For negated conditions of above pattern, it would be the other way around.

If the executing process IDs cannot be statically derived, the analysis tries to find out whether the condition can only evaluate to true for one process, e.g., a condition of form (`rank == i`), where i is an SV. At success, the analysis specifies nested operations by an `executionKind` of `One`. If above-mentioned is not possible, the `executionKind` of any nested operation is denoted by `Dynamic`.

3.2 SPMD IR

Special elements of an SPMD program are among others: process IDs, communicators representing a group of processes and context, process and communicator management, data management, and communication and synchronization operations. An SPMD program further involves the implicit execution of all operations by all processes, except branches depending on process IDs (multi-values). The idea is to have a minimal set of operations, types, and attributes in the SPMD IR that can cover those features.

Making use of the multi-level IR notion of MLIR, only the SPMD-related elements of the program are converted to the SPMD IR; the remaining, such as shared-memory parallelism induced by OPENMP, remain in its previous representation within MLIR. This allows multiple special-purpose IRs to coexist together in one representation and enables enhanced maintainability and ease of analysis for tool developers.

Table 2. Overview of the coverage of the SPMD IR for SPMD concepts.

Concept	Supported by	SPMD IR Operations
Process Management	MPI, SHMEM, NCCL	init, finalize, getSizeOfComm, getRankInComm, getDeviceInComm
Communicator Management	MPI, SHMEM, NCCL	commSplit, commDestroy, commSplitStrided, commWorld
Data Management	MPI, SHMEM, NCCL	malloc, realloc, free
Collective Comm.	MPI, SHMEM, NCCL	bcast, reduce, allreduce, scatter, reduceScatter, gather, allgather, alltoall, scan, exscan, barrier
Point-to-Point Comm.	MPI, NCCL	send, recv
Non-blocking Semantics (P2P and Collectives)	MPI, NCCL	wait{All,Some,Any}, test{All,Some,Any}

Table 3. Used types in the SPMD IR for SPMD-related concepts.

Description	Conceptually given in	Type in SPMD IR
Processor ID	MPI, SHMEM, NCCL	32-bit integer
Communicator	MPI, SHMEM, NCCL	spmd comm type
Communicated Data	MPI, SHMEM, NCCL	any memref type
Error or Success	MPI, SHMEM, NCCL	spmd error type
Reduce Operations	MPI, SHMEM, NCCL	spmd reduceOp type
Datatype	MPI, SHMEM, NCCL	spmd dataType type
Stream	NCCL	spmd stream type
Device ID	NCCL	32-bit integer
P2P Message Tag	MPI	32-bit integer
Request Handle (Non-blocking Comm.)	MPI	spmd req type
Status of a (Non-blocking) Operation	MPI, NCCL	spmd status type
Communicator Configuration	SHMEM, NCCL	spmd commConfig type

An overview of the operations and their categories in the SPMD IR is given in Table 2, of the types in Table 3, and respectively of the attributes in Table 1. When a concept is given in multiple programming models, the SPMD IR tries to unify the different calls into one operation. If a concept or concrete feature is given only in one programming model, e.g., `MPI_Scatter` in MPI or `shmem_team_split_strided` in SHMEM, then the SPMD IR would have its own operations for it. In case of different terms for the same concept or operation, the terminology of MPI is chosen due to its wider usage.

For instance, `MPI_Bcast`, `MPI_Ibcast`, `shmem_TYPENAME_broadcast`, `ncclBcast`, and `ncclBroadcast` are all represented by `spmd.bcast` (cf. Line 4 of Fig. 3). This operation takes the following operands: `comm` of type `spmd.comm`, `sendBuf` and `recvBuf` of type `memref`, `dataCount` of type `i64`, `datatype` of type `spmd.datatypeType`, `rootRank` of type `i32`, and optionally `stream` of type `spmd.streamType`. While the inherent attribute `isBlocking` accommodates for the non-blocking variant in MPI, the possibility of having separate send and receive buffer operands accommodates the SHMEM and NCCL not-in-place variants. The `spmd.bcast` operation further returns an optional request handle value of type `spmd.reqType` in case of being non-blocking and an error value of type `spmd.error`. The `stream` operand accommodates the NCCL variants that include GPU (programming) semantics.

While many SPMD features and API calls of the respective programming model could be mapped to one of the new SPMD IR operations without difficulty, certain differences among the models needed to be paid special attention.

Non-blocking Communication. In MPI, there are separate calls for blocking and non-blocking communication, and each of the non-blocking variants gets associated with a request handle to be used for explicit `wait` or `test` operations. In contrast, NCCL has no request handle and explicit `wait` operations, but it still has two ways of expressing non-blocking communication.

First, primitives to start and end a so-called group allow executing the calls in-between in a non-blocking way. Second, a communicator can be configured to be non-blocking, leading the `nccl` calls operating on it to be non-blocking. Especially the latter case might hide the information of being non-blocking from static analysis. Nonetheless, this work transforms `nccl` calls within a group to respective non-blocking SPMD IR operations and generates a `waitAll` operation waiting for all the created requests to be completed. Further, when the information is statically available, it moves the non-blocking information from the `nccl` communicator to the operations in the SPMD IR. Otherwise, the transformation falls back to the default case of blocking communication.

Another difference between both programming models is the query call for completion of non-blocking calls in `nccl`, namely `ncclCommGetAsyncError`. Although it is similar to `MPI_Test`, the problem is that the completion property is tied to the communicator and that it also forwards other errors encountered by the respective non-blocking call. This makes a static analysis and transformation difficult. In general, this operation could be mapped to `testAll` in the SPMD IR checking for the completion of all previously issued non-blocking communication calls. However, proper handling of this operation is deferred to future work.

Data Management. The SPMD IR provides three data management operations: `alloc`, `realloc`, and `free`. While all three programming models generally

```
1  %rank, %error1 = spmd.getRankInComm(%comm)
        {spmd.usedModel=0, spmd.execKind="All"}
2  %cmpRes = arith.cmpi eq (%rank, %c0) {spmd.execKind="All"}
3  scf.if (%cmpRes) {
4    %error2 = spmd.bcast (%comm, %sendBuf, %recvBuf, %count, %i32Type, %c0)
            {spmd.usedModel=0, spmd.isBlocking=true, spmd.executedBy=[0],
            spmd.execKind="Static"}
5  } {spmd.execKind="All", spmd.isMV=true}
```

Fig. 3. An exemplary excerpt of a program converted to the SPMD IR in MLIR. Some syntactical or IR constructs are left out or abbreviated for clarity.

support those functionalities and their API calls can be mapped to them, the semantics differ slightly. In SHMEM, **shmem_malloc** allocates memory on the so-called symmetric heap that reflects the PGAS notion of this programming model. Data used in SHMEM communication calls needs to be in this symmetric heap, except global and static variables. In contrast, MPI and NCCL treat the allocated memory as simply specially optimized for their communication calls (in MPI also used for the remote-memory access feature). Despite that, this work maps them to the same operations in the SPMD IR and thereby unifies the PGAS, distributed-, and accelerator-memory notions.

3.3   Workflow

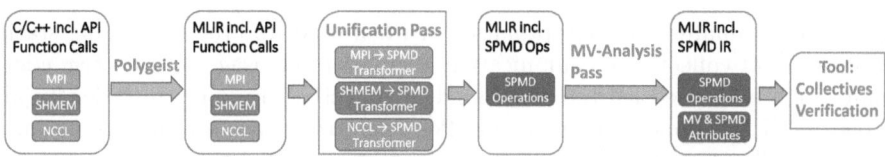

Fig. 4. The workflow of the proposed SPMD IR from an input program until a tool optimizing or verifying it, exemplarily shown for collectives verification.

Figure 4 shows the implemented workflow from a C/C++ program as input until a tool that makes use of the SPMD IR. The input possibly contains a combination of the currently supported programming models MPI, SHMEM, and NCCL. Polygeist then transforms the C/C++ program to a set of MLIR dialects, in which the library calls of the respective SPMD programming model are represented as external function calls (analogous to LLVM IR). For simplicity of the prototype, function calls are inlined at this step, inducing a current limitation for recursive functions. For NCCL, the prototype assumes a one-process-per-device mode.

The first compiler pass, called *unification pass*, converts the API function calls to the operations of the SPMD dialect and thereby unifies the library calls together with their arguments. In this pass, one transformer component is implemented for each programming model. For each newly created SPMD operation, an ID denoted by the `modelGroup` attribute tags all operations originating from the same programming model. For hybrid cases, this attribute can aid tools in certain analyses or for code generation. Attributes such as `isBlocking` or `isBuffered` in the SPMD dialect provide important static properties and differentiate among similar operations. It makes this kind of information readily available to a tool developer instead of hiding them behind the respective API calls.

The resulting IR should no longer contain specific data structures or external function calls to the library of the respective programming model. Instead, IR constructs of the SPMD dialect are present. If this state of the IR is already sufficient for a tool, it can stop here and proceed with it.

The second compiler pass, called *multi-value analysis pass*, applies the extended multi-value analysis introduced in Sect. 3.1. In result, it adds the attributes `isMultiValued`, `executionKind`, and `isExecuted(Not)By` to each operation where they apply.

An example of a program excerpt in the SPMD IR is given in Fig. 3. In Line 1, the process ID is obtained by the operation `spmd.getRankInComm`. Lines 2, 3, and 5 demonstrate how the multi-value `%rank` causes the condition of the `if` operation to be multi-valued, as the condition is whether the process ID equals zero. For that reason, the `spmd.bcast` operation in the `then` branch of the `if` operation in Line 4 is specified as being executed by process ID zero with an `executionKind` of `Static`.

4 Evaluation

This work evaluates the conceptualized SPMD IR and its prototype using static verification of collective communication. Here, correct usage of collective communication is defined as: the same kind of collectives is called in order by all processes of the same communicator. Possible error types are missing or mismatched calls or wrong program structures that may lead to deadlocks.

For that, this work reimplements PARCOACH's static approach [5,20] on the SPMD IR and assesses it by PARCOACH's micro-benchmark suite [5] and custom test cases available in MPI, SHMEM, and NCCL. In contrast to PARCOACH, all cases are first transformed to the SPMD IR, then the extended uniform multi-value analysis and thereon the collectives verification is conducted.

The goal of this evaluation is not to compete with PARCOACH on a production level, but to show that the proposed SPMD IR is suitable for such kind of analyses by having the same coverage on functionality-revealing test cases.

4.1 Extensions

This work further introduces two extensions to the static verification by PARCOACH. In general, PARCOACH iterates over LLVM IR for enumerating the collective calls by order and then trying to find multi-value dependent conditionals that decide on the execution of the set of collectives of same kind and order. If such conditionals can be found, an error is reported.

In particular, PARCOACH reports an error for any collective in a multi-valued loop or in a loop nested into a multi-valued branch operation. In contrast, the first extension differentiates static from dynamic cases and analyze the loop count when it is available at compile time. The collectives verification then uses this execution count and compares it with those of the matching collectives in the other branches of the control-flow graph. PARCOACH, however, only checks whether one of those matching collectives is contained in each control-flow path.

Second, for static cases where in the SPMD IR the executing processes of the matching collectives are known and the total number of executing processes specified, it is checked whether the matching collectives are executed by all processes. If successful, no error is reported for the given set of collectives.

4.2   Setup

The micro-benchmark suite consists of 15 codes written in MPI,[1] from which all could be ported to NCCL and 14 to SHMEM. The missing case is the non-blocking communication case, which is not supported in this form by SHMEM. The NCCL cases include MPI for the initial setup of it. Additionally, 14 test cases were designed and implemented to cover more functionality aspects of the multi-value analysis coupled with the collectives verification. One of them could not be ported to NCCL due to a missing explicit `wait` operation in NCCL. Further, 10 test cases were added for MPI to ensure coverage of the main collective calls that are not included in the other test cases. Extra eight hybrid cases should demonstrate MPI+NCCL, SHMEM+NCCL, and MPI+SHMEM usages.[2]

In total, 39 MPI codes are used in a direct comparison with PARCOACH. The results are categorized into four categories: True Positives, True Negatives, False Positives, and False Negatives. While a false positive is given when no error is present but reported, a true positive is given when the error is correctly reported. A false negative exists when an error is present but not reported, whereas, in a true negative there is no error and respectively not reported.

Software-wise, this work uses a patched Polygeist version at commit 4b04755 with a patched LLVM project incl. MLIR above LLVM 18 at commit 26eb428.[3] PARCOACH is used in its release version 2.42 [6]. For MPI, MPICH version 4.1.2 is used, for SHMEM Sandia (OPEN)SHMEM version 1.5.2, and for NCCL version 2.19.4. The concrete programming model implementations are relevant for the transformation from C/C++ to MLIR by Polygeist, especially for the programming-model-specific data structures.

---

[1] The original MPI codes from PARCOACH constituting the micro-benchmark suite can be found at: https://github.com/parcoach/microbenchmarks.

[2] All test cases, including individual results, and the implementation of the SPMD IR as a dialect, transformations, analyses, and collectives verification can be found at: https://github.com/RWTH-HPC/SPMD-IR-Paper-Code-Base.

[3] The sources are available at https://github.com/burakSemih/Polygeist/tree/spmd-ir-paper-eurompi-2024 (commit 49c2abd) for Polygeist and at https://github.com/burakSemih/llvm-project/tree/spmd-ir-paper-eurompi-2024 (commit 376bfa4) for the LLVM project.

4.3   Results

Figure 5 shows the results of running PARCOACH and respectively its port to the SPMD IR on the extended micro-benchmark suite. Both tools deliver the same classification for 37 of 39 MPI cases, including a correct error message. In contrast to PARCOACH, which does not support SHMEM or NCCL, a similar detection accuracy can also be observed on the SHMEM, NCCL, and hybrid cases for the SPMD IR verification.

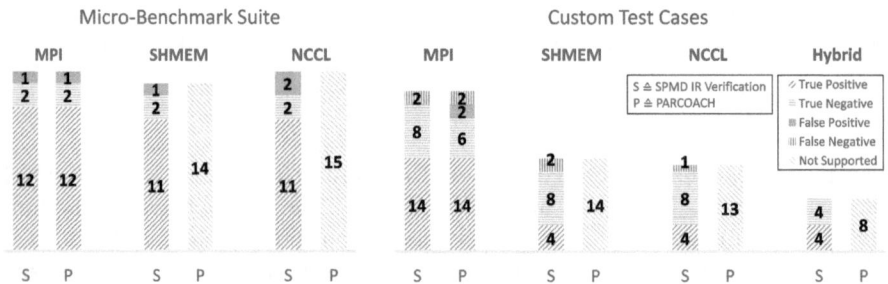

Fig. 5. The categorized results of PARCOACH compared with their approach ported to and extended on the SPMD IR for the static verification of collectives.

For the micro-benchmark suite, one additional false positive occurred only for the NCCL port of one test case, since the non-blocking communication is represented through group primitives instead of a different collective call kind. Consequently, the SPMD IR verification falsely does not match the two calls of originally same kind. This is a disadvantage of the abstraction introduced by the SPMD IR that could be solved, e.g., by introducing an attribute that distinguishes calls with a unique ID based on their original function calls. However, this would be contrary to the idea of the unification.

Within the new test cases, PARCOACH has two false positives for MPI, whereas the SPMD IR verification has respectively a true negative for all three programming models. One is due to the first extension of PARCOACH's analysis, i.e., by considering loop execution counts. The second is a static test case that is supposed to be called for four processes, and the IDs of the processes executing the collectives are known from the extended multi-value analysis reflected in the SPMD IR. This in turn is covered by the second extension.

One hybrid case that demonstrates the strength of having a unifying SPMD IR is given in Fig. 6. Lines 2 and 3 ensure that the processes obtain the same IDs in the equally sized world communicator/team of respectively MPI and SHMEM. Now, to properly detect the ordering error of the collectives between SHMEM and MPI (cf. Line 6–7 and Line 10–11), a tool needs to be capable of understanding SHMEM, MPI, and their hybrid usage. Since both programming models are transformed to the SPMD IR first, static analysis on this IR can understand effortlessly that Line 2 is in essence a duplication of MPI_COMM_WORLD with the

```
1   int myPE = shmem_my_pe();
2   MPI_Comm_split(MPI_COMM_WORLD, 0, myPE, &shmem_comm);
3   MPI_Comm_rank(shmem_comm, &myRank);
4   assert(myPe == myRank); // Ensured by Line 2 and 3
5   if (myRank == 0) {
6     shmem_int_sum_reduce(SHMEM_TEAM_WORLD, ...);
7     MPI_Bcast(..., shmem_comm);
8   }
9   else {
10    MPI_Bcast(..., shmem_comm);
11    shmem_int_sum_reduce(SHMEM_TEAM_WORLD, ...);
12  }
```

Fig. 6. A hybrid MPI+SHMEM example containing a collective communication error that is only detectable when understanding both programming models together.

ordering of SHMEM_TEAM_WORLD; only the IDs are unified. Therefore, shmem_comm and SHMEM_TEAM_WORLD are essentially the same communicator only accessible through different APIs. Having implemented this analysis, the SPMD IR verification detects this error.

5   Discussion

Although this work aimed to design the SPMD IR programming model independently, it is still rather MPI-centric. MPI is an extensive standard and programming model, has large community support, and is currently the de facto standard for distributed-memory programming. As a result, other programming models that focus on new features or different areas often align their design with MPI, or eventually, MPI incorporates their newly introduced functionalities. For example, NCCL is designed for inter-GPU communication and explicitly advertises an MPI-like interface. While SHMEM has a specific focus on one-sided communication, MPI introduced this set of functionality in form of remote memory access with MPI-2. Hammond et al. [3] showed that MPI-3 was sufficiently expressive to implement the SHMEM interface for collective and one-sided communication.

The difference from the scope of the IR compared to an MPI dialect in MLIR would be that the SPMD IR aims to accommodate multiple programming models from the beginning of its design. For example, MPI does not include GPU-specific semantics in its API calls, unlike NCCL's communication calls, which include a stream argument. Therefore, this stream argument is added as an optional operand to the respective SPMD IR operations. Static tools can then check if such an operand exists and depending on that include it in their analysis. The semantics of such additions that are not part of the MPI specification would be undefined and therefore not included by an MPI dialect.

Many calls and features of the selected programming models could be mapped to operations and attributes of the SPMD IR. However, certain differences, such as NCCL's non-blocking communication compared to MPI's, made it already difficult to universally unify programs statically without assumptions. Nonetheless, the goal would be to have such an IR that is sufficient for at least certain types of analyses, as it was shown for the collectives verification.

One disadvantage that comes along with the abstraction of the SPMD IR (or generally with any abstraction) is the loss of some information. For example, multiple former API calls can get a single call in the new representation. SHMEM's `fcollect` and `collect` calls both get mapped to an `spmd.allgather` operation. A similar case but with the non-blocking semantics in NCCL led to a false positive in the evaluation. Although a solution was sketched and it is always possible to introduce separate operations, such drawbacks need generally to be accepted as trade-offs for the increased extensibility and usability of the unification approach.

Furthermore, the attributes of the SPMD IR `executionKind`, `executed(Not)-By`, and `isMultiValued` provide useful static information not part of any of the parallel programming models' API call specifications. The evaluation showed that such analyses and reflection in the IR are useful and help to cover additional cases by separating dynamic from static cases. This could be indeed useful for target-specific generated code, such as by the PPL tool [22], where both the executing processes and the total number of processes are derivable at compile time. Currently, the respective analyses only support a few static patterns. Thus, future work should extend these analyses and explore additional use cases.

General application of the SPMD IR to other programming models such as NVSHMEM [14], GASPI [2], and UPC++ [27] should be possible and is planned for future work. It is also considered to support `Fortran` in addition to C/C++.

6   Related Work

Susungi and Tadonki conducted an extensive survey on IRs for explicitly parallel programs [24]. According to their observations, the majority of parallel IRs address shared-memory models, whereas only very few contributions apply to distributed-memory, host-accelerator-memory, and PGAS models.

With UPIR [28], Wang et al. propose a wide range of parallel IR constructs, specifying three parallelism patterns (SPMD, data and task parallelism), data attributes, explicit data movement, memory management, and synchronization operations. They have implemented a prototype in the source-to-source ROSE compiler and can export UPIR as an MLIR dialect. Although they follow the same idea of unifying different programming models as this work, their prototype only supports accelerator- and shared-memory models OPENACC [16] and OPENMP [17]. Further, their IR design does not abstract actual communication calls of different models to single operations but rather try to bring them as part of other constructs on an even higher level of abstraction. Lacking a proof-of-concept and evaluation particularly for distributed-memory and SPMD-like models, the feasibility of the necessary transformations for UPIR's high-level approach is unclear.

Another related approach is CIVL [23], a correctness verification tool based on model checking and symbolic execution. It introduces an IR called CIVL-C with the idea to abstract different programming models such MPI [10] or CUDA [15] to a single IR. While they provide common constructs for representing parallelism, they do not unify all the programming model specific API calls. Specifically, explicit communication is not part of their IR. For example, an MPI_Send remains an MPI_Send in their IR. CIVL-C therefore constitutes an IR on a different layer of abstraction compared to the SPMD IR.

There is an ongoing, early-stage effort for an MPI MLIR dialect [9]. However, it does not aim to cover the unification of different SPMD-like programming models or the necessary transformations to it. It also does not incorporate representing SPMD properties such as multi-valuedness, the execution kind, and executing processes of operations. Further, the SPMD dialect currently covers more core concepts of MPI together with the necessary transformations. Nonetheless, it could be used as an intermediate step between the transformation of API calls and the corresponding SPMD dialect operations once it is in more advanced state.

PARCOACH was originally introduced as a tool that verifies collective communication of MPI programs based on a static and an optional subsequent dynamic approach [20]. Although support for MPI+OPENMP [19], UPC [26], and CUDA [5] was added, its latest release versions [6] indicate that the tool is maintained and developed mainly for MPI; it was later extended to other error classes exclusively for MPI [12,21]. In contrast to the many model checking and dynamic verification tools such as CIVL or MUST [4], PARCOACH is one of the few tools relying on static analysis only and thereby allows a verification as part of an automatic compilation process. Since PARCOACH operates directly on programs reflected in LLVM IR, with MPI API calls represented as external function calls, adding support for another programming model would require altering the inherent analyses within the PARCOACH tool, in contrast to the extensibility of the SPMD IR verification.

7   Conclusion

This work presents an SPMD IR and MLIR dialect for the purpose of introducing an abstraction that allows programming-model-independent analysis and optimization. The SPMD IR currently encompasses the following features of SPMD programming models: process, communicator, and data management; collective and point-to-point communication; and non-blocking semantics (incl. synchronization operations). It further includes a set of attributes representing the results of the extended multi-value analysis, i.e., multi-valuedness of conditions, execution kind, and executing processes of operations.

An evaluation based on porting PARCOACH's static approach for verifying collectives to the proposed IR showed that the SPMD IR is both feasible to produce and expressive enough in terms of its level of abstraction. The prototype consisting of three compiler passes, a conversion pass of MPI, SHMEM, and NCCL to the unifying SPMD IR, an extended multi-value analysis, and the collectives verification, completes a full pipeline from C/C++ programs until verification.

The verification on the SPMD IR achieves the same coverage as PARCOACH on 37 of 39 MPI test cases of the extended micro-benchmark suite. Since for the SPMD IR verification same results can also be observed for their careful ports to

SHMEM and NCCL, it outperforms PARCOACH in terms of programming model support. Only the port of one test case to NCCL leads to a false positive, due to the level of abstraction introduced by the SPMD IR where it is no longer possible to distinguish different former function calls mapped to the same operation.

This paper further introduces two extensions to PARCOACH's approach allowing to cover two cases with true negatives instead of false positives by PAR-COACH. The SPMD IR's strength was additionally demonstrated on hybrid test cases with the combinations of MPI, SHMEM, and NCCL. The results make clear that the SPMD IR enables subsequent analyses to take place on a uniform representation so that working on hybrid programs is as difficult as on single-model codes. With the SPMD IR, support of other programming models can be achieved solely by extending the conversion compiler pass to the SPMD IR; the verification and multi-value analysis themselves do not need to be altered and demonstrate increased extensibility.

Since the evaluation of the prototype is based on micro-benchmarks, an assessment of the conversion to the SPMD IR and of the collectives verification would benefit from an application to more realistic codes such as proxy apps. Extending the SPMD IR to other SPMD features, such as remote memory access, and evaluating the IR by other use cases, e.g., another correctness-verifying or a performance-optimizing approach, is also part of future work.

Acknowledgement. The authors gratefully acknowledge the German Federal Ministry of Education and Research (BMBF) and the state government of North Rhine-Westphalia for supporting this work as part of the NHR funding. This work was supported by JST SPRING, Grant Number JPMJSP2106, and the RIKEN Junior Research Associate Program.

References

1. Aiken, A., Gay, D.: Barrier inference. In: POPL 1998 (1998)
2. GASPI Forum: GASPI: Global Address Space Programming Interface, Version 17.1 (2017). https://raw.githubusercontent.com/GASPI-Forum/GASPI-Forum.github.io/master/standards/GASPI-17.1.pdf. Accessed 26 July 2024
3. Hammond, J.R., Ghosh, S., Chapman, B.M.: Implementing OpenSHMEM using MPI-3 one-sided communication. In: OpenSHMEM 2014 (2014)
4. Hilbrich, T., Schulz, M., de Supinski, B.R., Müller, M.S.: MUST: a scalable approach to runtime error detection in MPI programs. In: Müller, M., Resch, M., Schulz, A., Nagel, W. (eds.) Tools for High Performance Computing 2009, pp. 53–66. Springer, Heidelberg (2010). https://doi.org/10.1007/978-3-642-11261-4_5
5. Huchant, P., Saillard, E., Barthou, D., Carribault, P.: Multi-valued expression analysis for collective checking. In: Yahyapour, R. (ed.) Euro-Par 2019. LNCS, vol. 11725, pp. 29–43. Springer, Cham (2019). https://doi.org/10.1007/978-3-030-29400-7_3
6. INRIA Researchers: PARCOACH - Git Repository, Release Version 2.42. https://github.com/parcoach/parcoach. Accessed 26 July 2024
7. Lattner, C., Adve, V.. LLVM. a compilation framework for lifelong program analysis & transformation. In: CGO 2004 (2004)

8. Lattner, C., Amini, M., Bondhugula, U., Cohen, A., et al.: MLIR: scaling compiler infrastructure for domain specific computation. In: CGO 2021 (2021)
9. Lydike, A.: RFC of an MPI Dialect in the LLVM Forum (2023). https://discourse.llvm.org/t/rfc-mpi-dialect/74705. Accessed 26 July 2024
10. Message Passing Interface Forum: MPI: A Message-passing Interface Standard, Version 4.1 (2023). https://mpi-forum.org/docs/mpi-4.1/mpi41-report.pdf. Accessed 26 July 2024
11. Moses, W.S., Chelini, L., Zhao, R., Zinenko, O.: Polygeist: raising C to polyhedral MLIR. In: PACT 2021 (2021)
12. Nguyen, V.M., Saillard, E., Jaeger, J., et al.: PARCOACH extension for static MPI nonblocking and persistent communication validation. In: Correctness 2020 (2020)
13. NVIDIA: NVIDIA Collective Communications Library (NCCL) Documentation, Version 2.19.3 (2023). https://docs.nvidia.com/deeplearning/nccl/archives/nccl_2193/user-guide/docs/index.html. Accessed 26 July 2024
14. NVIDIA: NVIDIA OpenSHMEM Library (NVSHMEM) Documentation, Version 2.8.0 (2023). https://docs.nvidia.com/nvshmem/archives/nvshmem-280/api/index.html. Accessed 26 July 2024
15. NVIDIA: CUDA Toolkit Documentation, Version 12.4. https://docs.nvidia.com/cuda/archive/12.4.0/. Accessed 26 July 2024
16. OpenACC Organization Members: The OpenACC Application Programming Interface, Version 3.3 (2022). https://openacc.org/sites/default/files/inline-images/Specification/OpenACC-3.3-final.pdf. Accessed 26 July 2024
17. OpenMP Architecture Review Board: OpenMP Application Programming Interface, Version 5.2 (2021). https://openmp.org/wp-content/uploads/OpenMP-API-Specification-5-2.pdf. Accessed 26 July 2024
18. OpenSHMEM Team: OpenSHMEM Application Programming Interface Specification, Version 1.5 (2020). http://openshmem.org/site/sites/default/site_files/OpenSHMEM-1.5.pdf. Accessed 26 July 2024
19. Saillard, E., Brunie, H., Carribault, P., Barthou, D.: PARCOACH extension for hybrid applications with interprocedural analysis. In: Knüpfer, A., Hilbrich, T., Niethammer, C., Gracia, J., Nagel, W.E., Resch, M.M. (eds.) Tools for High Performance Computing 2015, pp. 135–146. Springer, Cham (2016). https://doi.org/10.1007/978-3-319-39589-0_11
20. Saillard, E., Carribault, P., Barthou, D.: PARCOACH: combining static and dynamic validation of MPI collective communications. IJHPCA (2014)
21. Saillard, E., Sergent, M., Ait Kaci, C.T., Barthou, D.: Static local concurrency errors detection in MPI-RMA programs. In: Correctness 2022 (2022)
22. Schmitz, A., Burak, S., Miller, J., Müller, M.S.: Parallel pattern compiler for automatic global optimizations. Parallel Comput. (2024). https://doi.org/10.1016/j.parco.2024.103112
23. Siegel, S.F., Zheng, M., Luo, Z., Zirkel, T.K., et al.: CIVL: the concurrency intermediate verification language. In: SC 2015 (2015)
24. Susungi, A., Tadonki, C.: Intermediate representations for explicitly parallel programs. ACM Comput. Surv. (2021)
25. Tiotto, E., Pérez, V., Tsang, W., Sommer, L., et al.: Experiences building an MLIR-based SYCL compiler. In: CGO 2024 (2024)
26. UPC Consortium: UPC Language Specifications, Version 1.3 (2013). https://upc.lbl.gov/publications/upc-spec-1.3.pdf. Accessed 26 July 2024
27. UPC++ Specification Working Group: UPC++ Specification, Version 1.0 (2023). https://bitbucket.org/berkeleylab/upcxx/downloads/upcxx-spec-2023.9.0.pdf. Accessed 26 July 2024

28. Wang, A., Yi, X., Yan, Y.: UPIR: toward the design of unified parallel intermediate representation for parallel programming models. In: PACT 2022 (2023)
29. Zhang, Y., Duesterwald, E.: Barrier matching for programs with textually unaligned barriers. In: PPoPP 2007 (2007)

Annotation of Compiler Attributes for MPI Functions

Tim Jammer$^{(\boxtimes)}$ ⓘ, Adrian Schmidt, and Christian Bischof ⓘ

Technical University Darmstadt, Darmstadt, Germany
{tim.jammer,christian.bischof}@tu-darmstadt.de,
adrian.schmidt1@stud.tu-darmstadt.de

Abstract. This paper explores the use of LLVM IR function and parameter attributes to enhance compiler optimizations for code that uses MPI. As MPI is usually used as a dynamically linked library, the compiler is not able to automatically infer certain function attributes like `nofree`, which signals that no memory is deallocated in this function. Therefore, we implemented an LLVM compiler pass that annotates the used MPI functions with suitable attributes when compiling the user application. We manually derived applicable attributes based on the semantics described in the MPI standard, so that this approach is applicable to all MPI implementations.

We showcase different cases where this additional annotations impact the code generated by the compiler for the MiniApps from the Exascale Proxy Applications Project. The addition of MPI function annotations allows for a variety of compiler optimizations like reducing unnecessary memory accesses, optimizing register usage, and streamlining control flow.

The code of our annotation pass is available on GitHub: https://github.com/AdrSchm/mpi-attributes-pass.

Keywords: MPI · compiler analysis · compiler optimization · function attributes

1 Introduction

Many libraries for C and C++, including the MPI library, are used by including header files that contain function declarations and other definitions, and later linking against a precompiled library object file. Hence, when compiling applications that use them, the compiler only knows about the declarations, but not about the semantics of these functions. This prevents certain compiler optimizations that are possible when the compiler has more information, e.g. by the function being part of the same translation unit. Part of this lost information is the memory access behavior of functions, which is especially relevant when the function takes pointer parameters. Some of those pointers are used read-only, others may only be written to. Currently, the compiler does not have access to this information to perform optimizations and needs to assume that every

C. Blaas-Schenner et al. (Eds.): EuroMPI 2024, LNCS 15267, pp. 21–35, 2025.
https://doi.org/10.1007/978-3-031-73370-3_2

pointer is used for reading *and* writing. This results in the compiler needing to store the values of variables in memory before such function calls and reload them again afterwards. If the compiler knows additional access information, it may be able to keep values in registers instead, and thus use fewer memory accesses. Due to MPI being a library that relies heavily on the use of pointers, there are potentially many such opportunities for compiler optimizations in MPI applications.

A possible way to add information to the compilation process are compiler attributes. Adding attributes to declarations in header files provides compilers with some of the lost information, potentially enabling additional optimizations.

The idea of using compiler attributes between translation units is similar to the "Header Time Optimization" proposed by Moses and Doerfert, where they propagated the attributes inferred by the compiler to different translation units via annotations in the header file [10]. As Moses and Doerfert point out, more than half of the speedup achieved by using link time optimization (LTO) [6] can be obtained by only supplying the compiler with proper function attributes [10]. In our work, however, we do not use the compiler to infer the relevant function attributes, rather we infer them manually based on the MPI standards semantics.

In this paper, we investigate the effect that adding attributes to MPI functions has on the produced binaries of a selection of MiniApps. We investigate their impact on code generation, and how they enable formerly unused optimization possibilities.

The remainder of this paper is structured as follows: First, we provide an overview of the attributes we use in Sect. 2, and show how we annotate them to MPI functions. In Sect. 3, we showcase the differences of the generated assembly code with and without the annotations. Section 4 concludes our paper with a summary and an outlook on future work.

2   Attributing MPI Functions

We provide the compiler more information on the pointer usages of MPI functions by using LLVM IR function and parameter attributes. Usually, the compiler analyzes the function and infers the relevant attributes itself. But this only works inside of one translation unit. As the MPI library is usually dynamically linked at runtime, we need to specify the relevant annotations manually.

As the relevant attributes exist on the LLVM IR level, we implemented an LLVM optimization pass that annotates the definitions of the used MPI functions before all other optimizations happen. The attributes we employed are described in Sect. 2. Since these attributes are already part of the LLVM infrastructure, the usage of these attributes in order to perform code optimizations is already part of LLVM.

As can be seen in studies on MPI usage [5,8], most applications use only a small subset of the available MPI functions. Therefore, we currently limit the scope of our pass to such commonly used ones that are expected to be found in most MPI applications, such as point-to-point and collective operations.

2.1 Function and Parameter Attributes

As the MPI API extensively uses pointer arguments, and the memory access semantics is one of the key factors in possible compiler optimizations, we use the following relevant attributes:

memory This function attribute describes which memory locations are accessed in which way.[1] For our annotations we mostly use it as `memory(argmem: readwrite, inaccessiblemem: readwrite)`. The functions annotated in this way only access memory based on pointers given as parameters, or memory that the calling context has no access to, e.g. library internal buffers. Any other memory locations that are accessible from the calling context are not used by a function with this attribute, like for example captured pointers or other local variables. Therefore, it signals that memory related side-effects are possible, but not observable in the callers context unless those memory accesses happen through the function arguments. In contrast, `memory(readwrite)` indicates that accesses to arbitrary memory locations are possible, including those not happening through the arguments, but still observable in the callers context. Using this restriction allows for possible optimizations, as the compiler can be sure that variables that are not used during the call have the same value afterwards as they had before. It is possible to further specify the memory access behavior of individual parameters using the following attributes.

readnone This parameter attribute specifies that a pointer argument is not dereferenced during the function call. So variables do not have to be stored before and loaded afterwards, but can be kept in registers, for example.

readonly This parameter attribute specifies that a pointer argument is only dereferenced for reading the pointed to data. Pointed to variables need to be written to memory before the call, but they can potentially be kept in registers and used from there after the call.

writeonly This parameter attribute specifies that a pointer argument is only dereferenced for writing to the pointed to memory. This attribute describes that *if* a memory access happens it will be to only write data, but no guarantee that an access *will* happen. In rare cases this can omit stores to the memory region before function calls.

nocapture This parameter attribute specifies that a pointer argument is not captured by the function call. Capturing the pointer means that the function stores any bits of the pointer somewhere else, where they are accessible by other threads or functions even after the capturing function returns. These other threads or functions may be able to use this pointer for memory accesses or other operations, potentially modifying values that are used in other contexts. Other literature also use the term pointer *escape* for this [2]. In LLVM, `nocapture` implies *noescape* and these terms are used interchangeably, as there is no distinct attribute *noescape* [1]. Being sure that the pointer

---

[1] Since LLVM 16 this attribute replaces the attributes `argmemonly`, `inaccessible memonly` and `inaccessiblemem_or_argmemonly`.

is not captured and can therefore not escape, the compiler can omit memory
accesses after the function call, as there are no other threads or contexts that
may still have access the annotated pointer being able to modify the pointer's
content.

nofree This parameter attribute specifies that the memory pointed to by a
pointer argument is not freed during the call, so that accesses to the memory
locations are still valid afterwards. An identically named function attribute
extends this to all valid pointers in the calling context.

Other memory access related attributes of LLVM, such as **noalias**, are only
used to optimize the function body and are not relevant for optimization of the
code at the callsite. Thus, we focus only on the relevant attributes described
above.

2.2 Applying Attributes to MPI Functions

Inside one translation unit, the compiler can automatically infer some functions
and parameter attributes. In this work, however, we infer fitting attributes manually by analyzing the semantic of MPI functions as described in the standard
[9]. This approach allows for the annotation of additional attributes that the
compiler cannot infer by itself. This strategy is not dependent on any particular
MPI implementation, hence our pass is valid for any standard compliant implementation. We only annotate those pointers which are part of the MPI standard.
For an argument with the type `MPI_Comm` for example, OpenMPI uses a pointer,
while MPICH uses an integer. As both choices are in accordance with the standard, those arguments are not annotated. The following provides examples of
annotations for different MPI functions:

Utility functions such as `MPI_Comm_rank` or `MPI_Comm_size` read the status
of the MPI library. Those are annotated as follows:
`nofree memory(argmem: readwrite, inaccessiblemem: readwrite)`

`@MPI_Comm_size(%comm, ptr nocapture writeonly %size)` . The pointer
argument to this function is only written, which is why we annotate it with
`writeonly`. As the MPI library does not capture the pointer, we can also
annotate it with `nocapture`. The used `memory` attribute shows that no further
memory access occur. This function does not free any memory, so we annotate
it with `nofree` as well.

Blocking point-to-point operations are annotated as follows:
`nofree memory(argmem: readwrite, inaccessiblemem: readwrite)`

`@MPI_Send(ptr nocapture readonly %buf, %count, %dtype, %dest,`
`%tag, %comm)` According to the MPI standard, the used send buffer is only
read. Therefore, we annotate it as a `readonly` pointer. As this is a blocking
operation, it has completed once the call returns. Since the pointer to the
buffer is not used after the call returns, the `nocapture` attribute is appropriate. This attribute may not be inferred by the compiler alone. For the
compiler to be able to infer `nocapture`, it needs to *prove* that nothing cap-
tures the pointer. As the network might be involved in the communication,

the compiler may not be able to prove that all lower network layers do not capture the pointer. Since the call to `MPI_Send` does not free any memory accessible to the caller, we can annotate the whole function with `nofree` as well. The `memory` attribute, signalling no memory accesses to other reachable memory, is, strictly speaking, not a valid attribute for this function, or most other MPI functions for that matter. The reason is that it is possible to provide the MPI implementation with an additional user-allocated buffer which can then be used by the MPI library (buffered-mode). This buffer is potentially accessible from the user's program, which would require to use the attribute that *all* memory is `readwrite`. However, usage of a buffer supplied to the MPI library is undefined behavior according to the MPI standard's semantics. Therefore, for any compliant MPI application the user-provided buffer is effectively inaccessible to the user. This allows usage of the more restrictive memory attribute, potentially enabling more optimizations. Receive operations are annotated similarly, with `writeonly` being used instead of `readonly` for the buffer argument. The status parameter of a receive operation is annotated with `writeonly` and `nocapture`, as it is only written. Often it is `MPI_STATUS_IGNORE` [5] and thus not that important.

Non-blocking point-to-point operations have the same attributes as their blocking counterparts:

`nofree memory(argmem: readwrite, inaccessiblemem: readwrite)`

`@MPI_Isend(ptr nocapture readonly %buf, %count, %dtype,`

`%dest, %tag, %comm, ptr nocapture writeonly %request)`

The use of `nocapture` might look incorrect at first glance. Strictly speaking, the MPI library may capture the pointer to the send-buffer. But - similar to the above reasoning - the send-buffer pointer is"out of the user-application context" while the non-blocking operation is in progress, as any write usage can result in undefined behavior according to the MPI standard's semantics. For a send operation, read usages of the send-buffer are not harmful, but the semantics of MPI imply that the MPI library cannot write through the "captured" pointer. This means that assuming `nocapture` is also correct in those cases. Therefore, the compiler can treat non-blocking operation as "finished after the non-blocking call returns", as a standard compliant user application will not harmfully access the message buffer before it ensures completion with another MPI call.

Persistent operations are annotated as follows:

`nofree memory(argmem: readwrite, inaccessiblemem: readwrite)`

`@MPI_Send_init(ptr readnone %buf, %count, %dtype,`

`%dest, %tag, %comm, ptr nocapture writeonly %request)`

In this case, the message buffer is captured by the MPI library. The above reasoning does not apply, as the MPI library will use the captured buffer when the user instructs it to do so by using `MPI_Start`. As the initialization of a persistent request does not start communication, the buffer is annotated with `readnone`, as it is only going to be used later.

MPI_Start As this function starts the actual communication of a persistent request, we cannot specify any restrictions on the memory access of this func-

tion. The available attributes are not able to express any connections between
the communication request and the accessed buffers, as the same method is
used to start send and receive operations.

Collective operations have similar annotations as point-to-point operations:
`nofree` `memory`(argmem: `readwrite`, inaccessiblemem: `readwrite`)

`@MPI_Allreduce(ptr nocapture readonly %sendbuf,`
`ptr nocapture %recvbuf, %count, %dtype, %op, %comm)` Some collective operations can be specified to happen in-place by using `MPI_IN_PLACE` as
the send buffer. The compiler is able to detect the usage of this special MPI
pointer value and could theoretically adjust the annotations, based on which
pointers are read and which ones are written, by the given usage pattern.
This is not implemented in our pass yet, as it currently only supports annotations on a per-function level and it is possible to have some operations in
place and others with separate send and receive buffers. Therefore, our pass
uses the most conservative annotations that match usage of in-place operations as well as distinct memory regions, to limit the tool's complexity. The
`nocapture` attribute holds for both uses.

3   Evaluation

3.1   Impact on Exascale Proxy Apps

Our pass is not meant to be used when compiling an MPI library itself, but
intended to be included when compiling user applications that make use of the
library. To evaluate the impact of the additional added attributes, we employ
our pass during the compilation process of 14 MiniApps by the Exascale Proxy
Applications Project [3]. We tested all Proxy apps that use C or C++ and could
be built without the need for external dependencies.

In Fig. 1 we show how many MPI functions are annotated in the MiniApps.
Even though our pass only annotates the most used subset of all MPI functions, it covers most functions (68.2%) and callsites (77.2%) found in the Mini-
Apps. Some functions used in the MiniApps are not yet part of our pass, those
include functions to create derived MPI datatypes or communicators with topology information (e.g. `MPI_Cart_create`), as well as MPI I/O functions, as those
MPI functions are not used in the majority of MPI applications [5,8]. This can
also be seen in Fig. 1, considering that our pass annotates a majority of the used
MPI functions for a majority of the MiniApps.

We show the difference in the assembly instruction count of the resulting
binary in Fig. 2. For some apps like LULESH [7], the annotations optimize the
code in a way that leads to fewer instructions. For other apps like SimpleMOC [4],
the optimizations results in more instructions, due to code duplication performed
by the compiler when branches are eliminated, which was not possible without
the annotations.

Table 1. Comparison of annotated functions and callsites

	miniQMC	Kripke	PENNANT	Quicksilver	miniXyce	SimpleMOC	HPCCG	miniTri	Comb	LULESH	miniVite	miniAMR	hypar	sw4lite
Functions not annotated	0	2	0	5	1	5	2	7	15	3	14	4	10	14
Functions annotated	5	10	12	16	8	10	9	12	17	11	18	15	16	17
Callsites not annotated	0	2	0	5	1	10	7	7	24	17	47	8	18	127
Callsites annotated	7	16	19	16	30	23	34	57	54	125	96	149	194	103

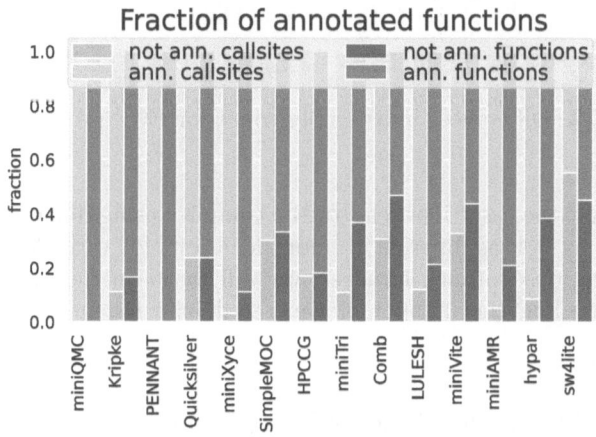

Fig. 1. Fraction of MPI Functions and callsites annotated. The left bar shows the fraction of the annotated functions. The right bar shows the fraction of annotated callsites. Table 1 shows the absolute values.

We detail the observable optimizations using the examples of LULESH [7] and SimpleMOC [4] in the following section. The other MiniApps trigger similar compiler optimizations.

3.2 Assembly-Level Differences

We compare the code generated without annotation from our pass with the assembly code generated including our pass. We use `clang` version 17.0.6 for the x86-64 architecture on a machine equipped with Intel Xeon Platinum 9242 CPUs running Red Hat 8.5.0–18 with openMPI version 4.1.6.

To be able to see additional optimizations we compile the programs using the respective default optimization flags, i.e. `O2` or `O3`, depending on the program. The memory access related optimizations discussed are part of the optimization level `O2`.

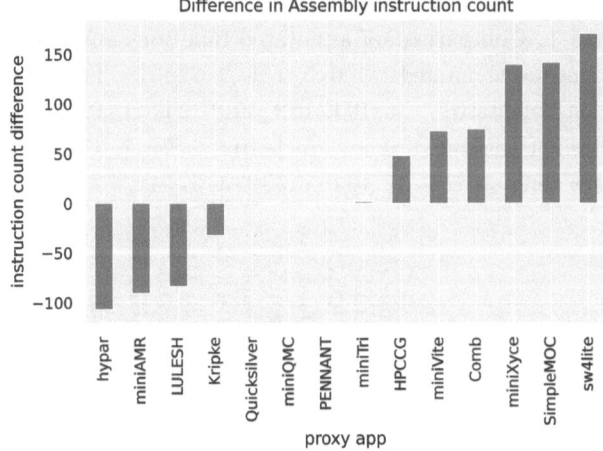

Fig. 2. Differences in assembly count for ECP proxy apps.

We note that the assertions lead to the compiler using different registers for computations, as well as different memory locations for variables on the stack. In the following observations however, we will focus on the more pronounced differences regarding the number of generated instructions and the resulting control flow.

Example: LULESH The left side of Listing 1 shows an excerpt of the original assembly generated, while the right side of Listing 1 shows the resulting assembly for the same source code location, when our annotation pass was enabled.

When comparing the assembly code in Listing 1, it is possible to observe the additional optimizations that are enabled by annotating attributes to the functions `MPI_Comm_size` and `MPI_Comm_rank`. In Line 9 in Listing 1, the generated assembly code loads the size of the communicator into a register. The optimized code (right in Listing 1) uses a different register, in order to reuse the communicator size from the register, which can be seen in Line 24 of Listing 1. In Line 13 of Listing 1, the previously initialized communicator rank is loaded from memory. As above, the un-optimized version (left in Listing 1) needs to re-load the same value from memory in Line 19.

As both of these values are reused again several times during the course of the entire program, our annotations result in 12 memory accesses being saved by this optimization.

The reason the compiler is able to perform these optimizations is the usage of the `nocapture` attribute, annotated to the pointer parameter of both `MPI_Comm_size` and `MPI_Comm_rank`. This attribute signals the compiler that the values of the `size` and `rank` variables stay the same. Without this attribute, the compiler needs to assume that the MPI library may change the variables

```
1    mov    rsi, rsp                    lea    rsi, [rsp + 76]
2    mov    rdi, rbx                    mov    rdi, rbx
3    call   MPI_Comm_size@PLT           call   MPI_Comm_size@PLT
4    lea    rsi, [rsp + 4]              lea    rsi, [rsp + 72]
5    mov    rdi, rbx                    mov    rdi, rbx
6    call   MPI_Comm_rank@PLT           call   MPI_Comm_rank@PLT
7    ; ...                              ; ...
8    ; Loads the value of size:         ; Uses separate register to load size:
9    mov    eax, dword ptr [rsp]        movsxd rbx, dword ptr [rsp + 76]
10   add    eax, 10                     lea    eax, [rbx + 10]
11   ; ...                              ; ...
12   ; Loads the value of rank:         ; Uses separate register to load rank:
13   mov    edx, dword ptr [rsp + 4]    mov    ebp, dword ptr [rsp + 72]
14   lea    rcx, [rsp + 20]             lea    rcx, [rsp + 12]
15                                      ; move between registers needed:
16                                      mov    edx, ebp
17   call   ;Mangled function name      call   ;Mangled function name
18   ; rank is reloaded:
19   mov    esi, dword ptr [rsp + 4]    ; Reuse of the loaded rank
20   mov    eax, dword ptr [rsp + ...]  mov    eax, dword ptr [rsp + 32]
21   or     eax, esi                    or     eax, ebp
22   ; ...                              ; ...
23   ; size reloaded from memory:       ; Reuse of the loaded size
24   mov    esi, dword ptr [rsp]        mov    esi, ebx
```

Listing 1. Comparison of assembly code generated from lulesh.cc with and without attributes. The left side shows the assembly generated without attributes. The right side shows the assembly generated with our pass enabled, which leads to the removal of unnecessary memory accesses, as indicated with the comments.

at any time, e.g. using a background thread and therefore needs to fetch the current value (again) before each usage.

Another exemplary difference is found in the produced assembly code generated from the code in Listing 2. Again, the compiler is able to perform additional optimizations because of the **nocapture** attribute annotated to the pointer parameter of MPI_Comm_rank. Despite the same attribute, the optimization is of a different kind. Essentially, the compiler is able to optimize the usage of variable i declared in Line 6 of Listing 2. As the compiler now knows that the value of myRank does not change, it can perform an index transformation on the inner loop by basically initializing i with myRank - 1. This will save the addition of i + myRank after the loop (Line 10 of Listing 2). This implies that the compiler keeps a copy of myRank - 1 on the stack, to use in the next iteration of the outer loop. Listing 3 shows a source code representation of the optimization done by the compiler. Due to other optimizations this does not cause an additional

```
1    int myRank;
2    MPI_Comm_rank(MPI_COMM_WORLD, &myRank);
3    // ...
4    while (regionNum == lastReg) {
5        regionVar = rand() % costDenominator;
6        i = 0; // loop index can be transformed to start at myRank
7        while (regionVar >= regBinEnd[i])
8            i++;
9        // a transformed index will save an addition in this line:
10       regionNum = ((i + myRank) % numReg()) + 1;
11   }
```

Listing 2: Excerpt of `lulesh-init.cc` from LULESH [7]

```
1    int myRank;
2    MPI_Comm_rank(MPI_COMM_WORLD, &myRank);
3    // ...
4    while (regionNum == lastReg) {
5        regionVar = rand() % costDenominator;
6        array_addr = &regBinEnd[0];
7        tmp = myRank - 1; // keep in register for outer while loop
8        do { tmp++; // increment is cheaper than reading from memory
9        } while (regionVar >= *array_addr++);// no implicit add in operator[]
10       regionNum = (tmp % numReg()) + 1; // at this point tmp equals myRank + i
11   }
```

Listing 3: Illustration of the idea for the optimization in Listing 2

addition in the inner loop even though Listing 3 looks like it. This fact is only observable when looking at the generated assembly directly.

Interestingly, the load instruction for initialization of i uses one byte less than the immediate-using instruction it replaces. Therefore, the compiler does not generate a subsequent padding in the machine code, which makes the code smaller and omits a following `nop` instruction.

Looking at a different part of LULESH, it is possible to see another effect of our annotated attributes. Listing 4 is an excerpt from a synchronization function that gets called for every simulated time step.

In Listing 4, the variable `fieldData` in Line 5 is an array of function pointers that is initialized earlier and effectively constant, as it is never written thereafter. Since the variable `xferFields` has the constant value of 6, the compiler is able to unroll the outer loop beginning in Line 4. This loop unrolling happens with and without our additional annotations. Ideally, the compiler should be able to statically resolve the function pointers and call the pointed-to functions in Line 7 directly. Compiling this program reveals that the compiler is not able to do this. The reason for this is that the compiler has no information on the MPI functions

```
1   if (planeMax) {
2       srcAddr = &domain.commDataRecv[pmsg * maxPlaneComm];
3       MPI_Wait(&domain.recvRequest[pmsg], &status);
4       for (Index_t fi = 0 ; fi < xferFields; ++fi) {
5           Domain_member dest = fieldData[fi];
6           for (Index_t i = 0; i < opCount; ++i) {
7               (domain.*dest)(dx*dy*(dz - 1) + i) = srcAddr[i];
8           }
9           srcAddr += opCount;
10      }
11      ++pmsg;
12  }
```

Listing 4: Excerpt of `lulesh-comm.cc` from LULESH [7]

called beforehand, namely `MPI_Wait` in Line 3 and `MPI_Comm_rank` in a line not shown. Therefore, it has to assume the worst case possible, which in these circumstances means that these functions modify the array contents to now point to different functions. Using our annotation pass, `MPI_Wait` and `MPI_Comm_rank` both get annotated with the `memory(argmem: readwrite, inaccessiblemem: readwrite)` attribute. By including this annotation, the compiler is able to determine that the array contents are indeed not modified and can statically resolve the function call. This only works in the first iteration however, as the called function itself is not marked with such attributes and therefore prevents further usage of this optimization. Since this is part of the internals of the application, additional attributes to the present MPI functions are not able to resolve this issue.

Nevertheless, even the single statically resolved function call causes major observable differences in the generated assembly. Since the function pointers point to member functions of a class, the compiler generates additional instructions to deal with the possibility of virtual function calls. The general idea is, that the compiler first need to check, if the pointer loaded from the array is a direct function pointer or a pointer to the virtual table. This is not necessary if the function pointer can be resolved directly. For the single resolved function pointer, the compiler is able to save 22 instructions in total. If the calls in the other iterations could be resolved as well, the same would apply to them.

Additionally, using the annotated attributes allows the compiler to keep other variables in registers, removing the need to reload values. In total there are another 5 memory accesses less during the execution of the rest of this unrolled loop.

Unfortunately, we were not able to measure a significant performance benefit of resolving the call to a direct one in the first loop iteration. As the application prevents resolving the calls in the other five iterations of the loop, the performance benefit is limited in this case.

Nevertheless, this shows that valuable optimizations can be triggered by the addition of relevant attributes to MPI functions. We see that the addition of attributes to MPI functions enables the compiler to statically resolve a function call to a direct one, which has the potential to enable further even more valuable optimizations, although they are not triggered in the case of LULESH. As our pass uses the attributes that are already part of the LLVM Infrastructure, it does not add any significant complexity to the toolchain. Considering that compiler optimizations are a difficult endeavor, huge performance improvements, without extra toolchain complexity are very difficult to realize. Therefore, we propose to use our pass to not let the optimization opportunities enabled by our pass unused, no matter how small they might be.

Example: SimpleMOC Another set of possible optimizations results in more instructions being generated. An example for this can be found when looking at the code in Listing 5, where several function calls to print routines are only made by the process with rank 0.

```
1   int mype = 0;
2   // ...
3   MPI_Comm_rank(MPI_COMM_WORLD, &mype);
4   // ...
5   if( mype == 0 )
6       logo(version);
7   // ...
8   if( mype == 0 )
9       print_input_summary(input);
10  // ...
11  for( int i = 0; i < num_iters; i++) {
12      // Loop code omitted
13      // Mainly this part gets duplicated
14      if( mype == 0 )
15          printf("keff = %f\n", keff);
16  }
17  // ...
18  if( mype == 0 ) {
19      border_print();
20      center_print("RESULTS SUMMARY", 79);
21      border_print();
22      // ...
23  }
```

Listing 5: Excerpt of `main.c` from SimpleMOC [4]

Due to the compiler having the additional information that the rank variable is not captured, it is able to eliminate branches. This is done by duplicating the code that is executed by all processes. In one of these duplicated regions the code specific for the process with rank 0 is included, whereas the other duplicated region does not have this code. In total, this omits three branches for processes with a rank different from 0, and several tests for the value of rank in the other region. The reason that this is not possible when compiling without our pass, is that the compiler has to assume that between different tests for the value of rank the value has been changed by a different thread or context, making multiple tests necessary. Knowing that the rank variable is not captured allows the compiler to omit these unnecessary tests. Separating both cases additionally allows the compiler to use 32 bytes less stack space as it is able to keep more values in registers.

Even though this optimization increases the size of the produced object file, fewer instructions are actually executed during runtime. As the code is only executed once in the initial setup of the application, the performance benefit is only minimal. However, this shows that such optimizations are possible, with the potential of a bigger impact when employing our pass on other programs.

Even though the performance improvement of this optimization is only minimal for the MiniApp, we can showcase that this kind of optimizations can lead to a substantial performance improvement by using an example program, designed to extract the effect of this optimization. The simple example[2] we used is shown in Listing 6. With this example, we are able to show a performance improvement of more than 16% (of 2.7 s) by annotating the MPI functions, as the information of the annotations allows the compiler to hoist the rank conditional from Line 7 of Listing 6 out of the loop.

```
1    int rank;
2    MPI_Comm_rank(MPI_COMM_WORLD, &rank);
3    starttime = MPI_Wtime();
4    for (int n = 0; n < num_iters; ++n) {
5      for (int i = 0; i < ARRAY_SIZE; ++i) {
6        array[i] = array[i] + (n * 42.1337); } // dummy calculation
7      if (n % ITER_TO_PRINT == 0 && rank == 0) {
8        printf("Iter %d : %f\n", n, array[0]); } // rank 0 prints progress
9      }
10   endtime = MPI_Wtime();
11   // Use MPI_Reduce to find the slowest process and report this timing
```

Listing 6: Example to showcase performance benefit

---

[2] The example is also part of our GitHub repository: https://github.com/AdrSchm/mpi-attributes-pass.

4   Conclusion

In this work we demonstrated that the compiler is able to further optimize applications using MPI, if it is provided additional information about the MPI functions. We supplied the compiler with this information via an LLVM compiler pass that annotates the used MPI functions with relevant attributes at the LLVM IR level. The attributes have been manually derived according to the MPI standards semantics. Thus, our approach is compatible with *all* standard-compliant MPI implementations.

We showed that the addition of attributes enables many different kinds of compiler optimizations, including the removal of unnecessary memory accesses and the simplification or elimination of branches.

The performance impact on the considered MiniApps of the Exascale Proxy Applications Project [3] is quite limited, as the optimizations mostly target the "management code" and not the core compute intensive part. As the runtime performance can only improve, and, depending on the interplay of MPI calls and the rest of the code, possibly in a substantial fashion, we advocate the use of these compiler attributes. Our approach does not add complexity to the LLVM infrastructure, as we employ well-established LLVM attributes.

Considering that the MPI Forum is currently discussing a standardization of an application binary interface (ABI) for MPI, we think that this work can inform ABI discussion by showcasing how compilers can leverage standardized information for code optimization.

In the future, we plan to investigate how the use of MPI wrapper functions influences the effects of added attributes. We also want to explore how the effects of the attributes are proliferated to other compiler environments. In particular, we want to explore how our findings can be transferred to Fortran applications, as Fortran can also be compiled with the LLVM toolchain. Additionally, we plan to extend our approach to also cover less frequently used MPI functions such as one sided operations.

The code of our annotation Pass is available on GitHub: https://github.com/AdrSchm/mpi-attributes-pass.

Acknowledgements. This work was supported by the Hessian Ministry for Higher Education, Research and the Arts through the Hessian Competence Center for High-Performance Computing and by the Federal Ministry of Education and Research (BMWF) and the states of Hesse as part of the NHR program. Measurements for this work were conducted on the Lichtenberg high performance computer of the TU Darmstadt.

References

1. LLVM Language Reference Manual (2024). https://llvm.org/docs/LangRef.html#pointercapture. Accessed 04 May 2024
2. Choi, J.D., Gupta, M., Serrano, M., Sreedhar, V.C., Midkiff, S.: Escape analysis for Java. ACM Sigplan Not. **34**(10), 1–19 (1999)

3. Exascale Computing Project: Exascale proxy applications (2022). https://proxyapps.exascaleproject.org/. Accessed 23 Apr 2024
4. Gunow, G., Tramm, J., Forget, B., Smith, K., He, T.: SimpleMOC – a performance abstraction for 3D MOC. In: ANS & M&C 2015 - Joint International Conference on Mathematics and Computation (M&C), Supercomputing in Nuclear Applications (SNA) and the Monte Carlo (MC) Method (2015)
5. Hück, A., Jammer, T., Protze, J., Bischof, C.: Investigating the usage of MPI at argument-granularity in HPC codes. In: Proceedings of EuroMPI2023: the 30th European MPI Users' Group Meeting, EuroMPI2023, pp. 1–10. ACM (2023). https://doi.org/10.1145/3615318.3615322
6. Johnson, T., Amini, M., Li, X.D.: ThinLTO: scalable and incremental LTO. In: 2017 IEEE/ACM International Symposium on Code Generation and Optimization (CGO), pp. 111–121. IEEE (2017)
7. Karlin, I., Keasler, J., Neely, R.: Lulesh 2.0 updates and changes. Technical Report. LLNL-TR-641973 (2013)
8. Laguna, I., Marshall, R., Mohror, K., Ruefenacht, M., Skjellum, A., Sultana, N.: A large-scale study of MPI usage in open-source HPC applications. In: Proceedings of the International Conference for High Performance Computing, Networking, Storage and Analysis, SC 2019. Association for Computing Machinery, New York (2019). ISBN 9781450362290. https://doi.org/10.1145/3295500.3356176
9. Message Passing Interface Forum: MPI: A Message-Passing Interface Standard Version 4.1 (2023). https://www.mpi-forum.org/docs/mpi-4.1/mpi41-report.pdf
10. Moses, W., Doerfert, J.: "Header Time Optimization": cross-translation unit optimization via annotated headers (2020). https://c.wsmoses.com/posters/HTO_Poster.pdf. Accessed 23 Apr 2024

Limitations and Extensions for GPGPUs in MPI

Understanding GPU Triggering APIs for MPI+X Communication

Patrick G. Bridges[1]([✉]) [iD], Anthony Skjellum[2] [iD], Evan D. Suggs[2] [iD],
Derek Schafer[1] [iD], and Purushotham V. Bangalore[3] [iD]

[1] University of New Mexico, Albuquerque, NM 87131, Mexico
{patrickb,dschafer1}@unm.edu
[2] Tennessee Technological University, Cookeville, TN 38505, USA
{askjellum,esuggs}@tntech.edu
[3] The University of Alabama, Tuscaloosa, AL 35401, USA
pvbangalore@ua.edu

Abstract. GPU-enhanced architectures are now dominant in HPC systems, but message-passing communication involving GPUs with MPI has proven to be both complex and expensive, motivating new approaches that lower such costs. We compare and contrast stream/graph-, kernel-triggered, and GPU-initiated MPI communication abstractions, whose principal purpose is to enhance the performance of communication when GPU kernels create or consume data for transfer through MPI operations. Researchers and practitioners have proposed multiple potential APIs for GPU-involved communication that span various GPU architectures and approaches, including MPI-4 partitioned point-to-point communication, stream communicators, and explicit MPI stream/queue objects. Designs breaking backward compatibility with MPI are duly noted. Some of these strengthen or weaken the semantics of MPI operations. A key contribution of this paper is to promote community convergence toward common abstractions for GPU-involved communication by highlighting the common and differing goals and contributions of existing abstractions. We describe the design space in which these abstractions reside, their implicit or explicit use of stream and other non-MPI abstractions, their relationship to partitioned and persistent operations, and discuss their potential for added performance, how usable these abstractions are, and where functional and/or semantic gaps exist. Finally, we provide a taxonomy for these abstractions, including disambiguation of similar semantic terms, and consider directions for future standardization in MPI-5.

Keywords: Stream-triggered message passing · Kernel-triggered message passing · GPU-initiated message passing · MPI · GPU · MPI | X · partitioned communication

1 Introduction

Most MPI implementations now include support for GPU data paths, enabling standard MPI host-based APIs to move data to and from GPU memory. This

C. Blaas-Schenner et al. (Eds.): EuroMPI 2024, LNCS 15267, pp. 39–55, 2025.
https://doi.org/10.1007/978-3-031-73370-3_3

feature is generally termed *GPU-aware MPI* and significant progress has been made toward standardizing this implementation feature through work on *MPI memory types* [13]. Importantly, the MPI operation stages of *initialization, starting, completion,* and *freeing* [12][1] are all conducted by code running on the host CPU in this approach; GPU code that needs to cause or coordinate MPI operation state changes must do so indirectly by synchronizing with CPU code that makes those updates on behalf of the GPU code.

Integrating MPI into GPU *control paths* is also important because it could eliminate the GPU/host communication latencies in current MPI implementations. This is a more challenging problem since it requires addressing multiple complex issues, including:

- Which GPU control paths (stream execution and kernel execution) should support interacting with MPI operations?
- To what degree can current MPI abstractions be reused on GPU control paths?
- What are the concurrency semantics of MPI operations on host and GPU control paths?

The myriad proposed approaches for addressing these issues [1,3,5,11,12,14, 15,17,18] have focused on *GPU-triggered communication APIs* in which host calls initialize and free MPI communication requests and the GPU control path starts and in some cases completes MPI communication requests. When the GPU control path used for starting and completion is the GPU stream scheduler, here and elsewhere this is termed *stream-triggered communication* and generally does not involve GPU-callable routines; instead the host API interacts with the GPU stream control program to schedule implicit GPU starting and completion of communication operations. In contrast, using GPU kernel thread execution for starting and completion is generally termed *kernel-triggered communication* and requires the addition of explicit GPU-callable APIs for starting and completing communication. As opposed to these options, Intel's approach includes *GPU-initiated APIs* (in which all parameters to the operation are provided in the GPU) and *GPU-synchronization APIs* [9,10].

Despite the many proposals, there is neither a consensus nor standard, either formal or informal, on an appropriate MPI API for GPU-triggered communication. To provide information and guidance for the MPI community to systematically address this issue (such as in MPI-5, or ideally sooner), this paper collects, organizes, and summarizes information about the various proposed MPI GPU-triggered communication approaches and highlights their similarities and differences. After providing background on representative GPU communication triggering proposals (Sect. 2), this paper makes the following contributions:

- Presents a taxonomy for approaches to GPU-triggered communication that highlights the major design decisions that an MPI API needs to address (Sect. 3);

---

[1] The term 'initiating' refers to a sequence of the initialization and starting phases.

- Summarizes the key features of and classifies nine different MPI stream- and kernel-triggering API proposals using this taxonomy and compares and contrasts key requirements and API design elements of these approaches (Sect. 4);
- Highlights key gaps in the existing GPU triggering MPI APIs and in the MPI standard that will need to be addressed by future proposals for a robust MPI GPU triggering API (Sect. 5).

Finally, the paper offers conclusions and recommends a path forward in Sect. 6.

2   Representative GPU-Triggered Communication Abstractions

To illustrate the wide range of design choices and challenges in this area, we begin by providing information on four proposals for GPU-triggered MPI communication. Specifically, we discuss the stream triggered, two-sided communication support in recent MPICH implementations [18], the stream-triggered MPI one-sided communication support recently proposed by researchers at Hewlett Packard Enterprise (HPE) [15], extensions to the MPI 4.0 Partitioned Communication interface [12] to support GPU kernel triggering of MPI communication [8], as well as the GPU-initiated model proposed by Intel [9,10].

We also present simple ping-pong communication for each proposal to further elucidate their proposed approaches. Together, this section highlights and provides essential background on the diverse design choices we explored in designing the GPU triggered communication taxonomy described below in Sect. 3.

2.1   MPICH Triggering

The GPU triggering support in recent MPICH implementations [18] focuses on stream triggering of MPI communication using two abstractions:

MPIX_Stream – an MPI object to sequence MPI operations and to which external execution contexts, for example GPU streams, can be bound. This provides clearly defined concurrency semantics for MPI operations in multiple execution contexts including multi-threaded host execution contexts and accelerator-based MPI+X environments; and,

GPU Stream communicators – MPI communicators to which an MPIX_-Stream object is attached to a GPU stream execution context, and on which MPI operations are enqueued to the attached GPU stream and return immediately in the host execution context.

MPICH provides explicit enqueue variants of the supported GPU-triggered operations that return immediately to the host; GPU synchronization routines must be used to await for completion of these operations on the GPU. MPICH implementers considered making MPI_Send and MPI_Recv on communicators with GPU streams attached have enqueue semantics (similar to the previously proposed MPI-GDS API [17]), but in the end rejected this because it would change the semantics of well-known MPI APIs. Finally, MPICH stream communicators also include additional features to support APIs similar to the previous MPI Endpoints proposal [2].

```
1   MPIX_Stream mpistream;
2   MPI_Comm stream_comm;
3   MPI_Info info;
4
5   MPI_Info_create(&info);
6   MPI_Info_set(info, "type", "cudaStream_t");
7   MPIX_Info_set_hex(info, "value", &cudastream,
8                     sizeof(cudastream));
9   MPIX_Stream_create(info, &mpistream);
10  MPI_Info_free(&info);
11  MPIX_Stream_comm_create(MPI_COMM_WORLD, mpistream,
12                     &stream_comm);
13
14  for (int i = 0; i < niters; i++) {
15    if (my_rank == 0) {
16      MPIX_Send_enqueue(src_buf, 1, MPI_INT, 1, 123,
17                     stream_comm);
18      MPIX_Recv_enqueue(src_buf, 1, MPI_INT, 1, 123,
19                     stream_comm, MPI_STATUS_IGNORE);
20    } else if (my_rank == 1) {
21      MPIX_Recv_enqueue(dst_buf, 1, MPI_INT, 0, 123,
22                     stream_comm, MPI_STATUS_IGNORE);
23      MPIX_Send_enqueue(dst_buf, 1, MPI_INT, 0, 123,
24                     stream_comm);
25    }
26  }
27  cudaStreamSynchronize(cudastream);
```

Fig. 1. Stream-triggered MPI Ping Pong using MPICH Stream Triggering [18]

Figure 1 shows an example ping-pong communication using this interface. We highlight the following key features of this example:

- To use GPU stream-triggered communications, the programmer must create a new communicator;
- The stream communicator concept, similar to the one previously proposed for MVAPICH [17], can be naturally extended to include additional operations beyond the point-to-point operations supported in the current implementation, including collective communications; and,
- MPICH's stream communicators enqueued operations require that the calling process must explicitly synchronize with the underlying GPU stream using GPU-specific operations to ensure completion of the corresponding MPI operation in the GPU execution context.

2.2   HPE One-Sided

The HPE one-sided GPU triggering API [15] supports stream-triggered, one-sided communication[2]. The stream abstractions included in HPE's approach rely on GPU-NIC asynchronous stream triggering that integrates the NIC command queue and the GPU stream. In this approach, the CPU puts commands in the Cray Cassini NIC's command queue and then GPU stream operations triggers these commands. This removes unnecessary synchronization on the CPU. HPE's one-sided API is designed to allow for GPU-NIC progress where the host CPU is fully bypassed in progressing communication. HPE's previous two-sided GPU triggering APIs [14] required host progress to receive messages because of the need for tag matching and unexpected message handling.

```
 1   /* Normal MPI communicator, window, group, and  */
 2   /* buffers assumed to exist  */
 3   for(int i = 0; i < niters; i++) {
 4     if(rank == 0){
 5       /* Send ping */
 6       MPI_Win_start(group, MPI_MODE_STREAM, win);
 7       MPI_Put(src,n,MPI_INT,1, disp, n, MPI_INT,win);
 8       /* Puts triggered here */
 9       MPIX_Win_complete_stream(win,stream);
10       /* Receive pong */
11       MPIX_Win_post_stream(group, win, stream);
12       MPIX_Win_wait_stream(win,stream);
13     } else { /* Receive ping */
14       MPIX_Win_post_stream(group, win, stream);
15       MPIX_Win_wait_stream(win, stream);
16       /* Send pong */
17       MPI_Win_start(group, MPI_MODE_STREAM, win);
18       MPI_Put(src, n, MPI_INT, 0, disp, n, MPI_INT,win);
19       /* Puts triggered here */
20       MPIX_Win_complete_stream(win, stream);
21     }
22   }
23   cudaStreamSynchronize(stream);
```

Fig. 2. Stream-triggered MPI Ping Pong using HPE One-Sided Stream Triggering

Figure 2, shows an example of a one-sided ping-pong test using the HPE Cray MPI interface where stream-triggered variants of window post, wait, and complete operations are combined with window start and put operations to achieve fully offloaded GPU communication. We highlight the following key features of this example:

---

[2] HPE also provides stream-triggered, two-sided communication, not considered here.

- One-sided communication mixes new `MPIX_*` functions and standard MPI functions, because the *Window* is associated with the stream.
- `MPI_Put` and `MPI_Win_start` do not have stream-triggered `MPIX_` alternatives and simply initialize future communications operations to be triggered by the stream-triggered complete operation.
- The `MPI_Win_complete_stream` starts communication operations in the command queue initialized by the host (e.g., using `MPI_Put`). This utilizes the GPU and NIC without weakening MPI RMA synchronization semantics, and in reality requires *stronger* MPI RMA synchronization semantics by *always* deferring one-sided operations until `MPI_Win_complete_` stream is executed by the GPU stream control program. That is, in the HPE one-sided API, the communications indicated by `MPI_Put` calls *cannot* legally occur until `MPI_Win_complete_stream` is executed in stream order by the GPU control program.

2.3   Kernel-Triggered Partitioned Communication

The MPI-ACX implementation [1] includes a prototype of the partitioned communication detailed in MPI-4. Partitioned point-to-point communication was specifically added to MPI-4 for a variety of reasons, including providing matching semantics (matching at initialization) and lightweight interfaces for data transfer initiation[3]. A specific nuance in this approach is that both `MPIX_ Parrived` and `MPIX_Pready` can be called from the host and the CUDA device. There are device-variants of the host requests to support the device-invoked operations.

Notably, the completion of an `MPI_Psend_init` call does not guarantee that a receiver has been matched prior to calling `MPI_Start`; it can instead occur at the first `MPI_Wait` for both sides of the partitioned channel. As such, proposals were offered for MPI-4.1 denoted `MPI_Pbuf_prepare` to guarantee initialization completion prior to first use and ensure readiness of buffers upon reuse [6]. This has not yet been adopted for the standard, but appears essential to avoid unexpected messages that would introduce complex logic that is considered untenable in GPU kernels.

Figure 3 details a ping-pong test based on the ring program supplied with MPI-ACX; and the following are some key observations:

- In MPI-ACX, the programmer uses `MPIX_Request` to create a `MPIX_Prequest` for the device to use in operations. These objects are tied to each other with SPSVERBc21SPSVERBc23.
- The host-based MPI request object is used for regular MPI functions such as `MPIX_Start` and `MPIX_Wait`.
- Different request types and function signatures are needed for GPU and CPU interfaces due to differences between the state needed in each context.

---

[3] It also removes the restrictions of persistent send and receive operations—`MPI_Send_init` and `MPI_Recv_init`—from MPI-1, which are forbidden to communicate and do not match only once. These fail to offer a channel semantic or obviate receive-queue matching. By way of contrast, single partitioned mode provides a unidirectional channel abstraction.

```
1  __global__ void ready(MPIX_Prequest preq) {
2    MPIX_Pready(threadIdx.x, preq);
3  }
4
5  __global__ void arrived(MPIX_Prequest preq) {
6    int flag = -1;
7    for(;;){
8      MPIX_Parrived(preq, threadIdx.x, &flag);
9      if(flag) break;
10   }
11 }
12
13 void pingpong(...) {
14   int sendbuf[1], recvbuf[1];
15   MPIX_Request srequest, rrequest;
16   MPIX_Prequest psrequest, prrequest;
17   int otherrank = (rank == 0) ? 1 : 0;
18   MPIX_Psend_init(sendbuf, 1, 1, MPI_INT, otherrank, 0,
19                   MPI_COMM_WORLD, MPI_INFO_NULL,
20                   &srequest);
21   MPIX_Precv_init(recvbuf, 1, 1, MPI_INT, otherrank, 0,
22                   MPI_COMM_WORLD, MPI_INFO_NULL,
23                   &rrequest);
24   MPIX_Prequest_create(srequest, &psrequest);
25   MPIX_Prequest_create(rrequest, &prrequest);
26   for(int i = 0; i < maxiters; i++) {
27     MPIX_Start(&rrequest); // ping if rank==1, else pong
28     MPIX_Start(&srequest); // pong if rank==1, else ping
29     if(rank == 0) {
30       ready<<<1, 1, 0, 0>>>(psrequest);
31       MPIX_Wait(&srequest, MPI_STATUS_IGNORE);
32       arrived<<<1, 1, 0, 0>>>(prrequest);
33       MPIX_Wait(&rrequest, MPI_STATUS_IGNORE);
34     } else {
35       arrived<<<1, 1, 0, 0>>>(prrequest);
36       MPIX_Wait(&rrequest, MPI_STATUS_IGNORE);
37       ready<<<1, 1, 0, 0>>>(psrequest);
38       MPIX_Wait(&srequest, MPI_STATUS_IGNORE);
39     }
40   }
41 }
```

Fig. 3. MPI Ping Pong using MPI-ACX Partitioned Stream Triggering

2.4   Intel GPU-Initiated Communication

Intel provides a GPU-initiated communication feature [10] that appears similar
to HPE's one-sided communication prototype. Intel's additions to its MPI implementation [9] is kernel-triggered, and uses existing SYCL queues for communi-

cation ordering instead of an explicit MPI ordering object (as MPICH does). Figure 4 demonstrates the ping-pong exemplar following Intel's approach that reduces the number of MPI functions to only `MPIX_Put_notify` and `MPIX_Win_get_notify` instead putting work on the GPU using a SYCL queue object and adding them as events[4].

3   A Taxonomy of MPI GPU-Triggered Communication

Based on a careful examination of both the MPI standard and prior proposals for GPU-triggered communication, we defined the following categories for classifying key characteristics of MPI GPU-triggered communication proposals in four different overarching areas:

Area 1: GPU control path used: Does the API support the GPU stream control path or kernel control path for starting and completing MPI communication operations? In the case of APIs where both stream- and kernel-triggering are supported, we split the API into separate stream- and kernel-triggered sub-APIs and classify them separately because of the frequent semantic and API differences between the such approaches in other categories.

Area 2: API Design Considerations

Reuses Existing MPI APIs or abstractions: Does the GPU-triggering API reuse existing MPI communication operations or abstractions to enable GPU triggering of communication operation starting or completion, or does it instead create new MPI operations or abstractions?

Changes Existing MPI API Semantics: If the API reuses existing APIs or abstractions, does it change the semantics of these API elements to behave differently than they currently do? For proposals that modify the API, we classify whether the API *strengthens* MPI API semantics in a way that preserves backward compatibility or *weakens* MPI semantics in a way that may compromise backward compatibility.

Separate MPI Operation Initialization and Starting: Does the API use a single call to execute the *initiate* stages of MPI communication operations or does it separate this into explicit API calls to *initialize* and *start* MPI communication operations?

GPU MPI Operation Completion Support: Does the API support GPU detection of the completion of GPU-initiated MPI operations? We identify the classifications of *all*, *some*, and *none* for this category, corresponding to GPU control paths supporting waiting or polling for the completion of (1) all GPU-initiated MPI operation, (2) some GPU-initiated MPI operations, or (3) requiring host code to wait or poll for the completion of MPI operations.

Collective Communication Support: Does the API specify operations enabling a single GPU communication operation to communicate with multiple processes? We classify collective support as either *full*, *partial*, *group*, or

---

[4] Personal Communication, Dr. Daniel J. Holmes, Intel Corp., June 14, 2024.

```
 1 void do_pingpong_mpi(int target, sycl::queue &q, [[
     maybe_unused]] void **ptrs, int threads=1) {
 2     double latency = 0.0;
 3     int tgt = target;
 4     MPI_Win_fence(0, win);
 5     for (int i=0; i<2;++i) {
 6         int iter = iters[i];
 7         if (rank == 0) {
 8             sycl::event e = q.submit([&](sycl::handler &h)
                 {
 9                 h.parallel_for_work_group(sycl::range(1),
                     sycl::range(threads), [=](sycl::group
                     <1> grp) {
10                     grp.parallel_for_work_item([&](sycl::
                         h_item<1> item) {
11                         int id = item.get_global_id(0);
12                         int v = 0;  MPI_Count c = 0;
13                         for (int i=1; i<iter; ++i) {
14                             MPIX_Put_notify(&v, 1, MPI_INT
                                 , tgt, id, 1, MPI_INT, id,
                                 win);
15                             while (c<i)
16                                 MPIX_Win_get_notify(win,
                                     id, &c);
17                         }   });   });   });
18             q.wait();
19         } else if (rank == target) {
20             q.submit([&](sycl::handler &h) {
21                 h.parallel_for_work_group(sycl::range(1),
                     sycl::range(threads), [=](sycl::group
                     <1> grp) {
22                     grp.parallel_for_work_item([&](sycl::
                         h_item<1> item) {
23                         int id = item.get_global_id(0);
24                         int v = 0; MPI_Count c = 0;
25                         for (int i=1; i<iter; ++i) {
26                             while (c<i)
27                                 MPIX_Win_get_notify(win,
                                     id, &c);
28                             MPIX_Put_notify(&v, 1, MPI_INT
                                 , 0, id, 1, MPI_INT, id,
                                 win);
29                         }   });   }).wait();
30         }   }
31     MPI_Win_fence(0, win);
32     for (i = 0; i < threads; ++i)
33         MPIX_Win_set_notify(win, i, (MPI_Count)0);
34 }
```

Fig. 4. Ping Pong using Intel GPU-Initiated MPI [9,10]

none, corresponding to (1) an API that supports the full semantics of MPI two-sided collective operations, (2) an API that supports a subset of the MPI two-sided collective operations, (3) an API that supports collective pairwise exchanges between subgroups of a communicator such as one-sided group or two-sided neighbor collectives, or (4) no specified support for collective communication.

Area 3: Ordering and Concurrency Considerations

MPI Operation Sequencing Abstraction: Does the API include an explicit MPI abstraction or object for ordering GPU communication operations separate from GPU-provided abstractions?

Sequencing Abstraction Semantics: If the API includes an explicit sequencing abstraction, are communication operations sequenced using it fully ordered or partially ordered (e.g., using a fencing or graph abstraction)?

Specification of MPI Concurrency Standard Integration: Does the API address concurrency-related issues arising from GPU triggering of MPI communication through *explicit* specification or *implicit* specification via the existing MPI *thread multiple* mode, or are concurrency semantics *unspecified*?

Area 4: Implementation Considerations

GPU/NIC Progress: Does the API enable message initiation or starting and completion by the GPU and network device without the involvement of the host CPUs? This is generally accomplished by supporting one-sided data movement that avoids the control flow complexity of matching in the receive path.

Available Implementation or Evaluation: Is an implementation or evaluation of this API available either for download and installation, from a vendor, or in a peer-reviewed publication so that it can potentially be tested or compared with other APIs?

Multi-architecture Support: Does the implementation, if available, target a single vendor architecture or has it been demonstrated for multiple GPU and/or NIC accelerator architectures? We categorize an implementation as *Yes* when it supports multiple GPUs and network architectures, as *GPU* or *NIC* when it has been demonstrated on multiple GPU or NIC architectures, respectively, and as *No* when it has been demonstrated on neither multiple NIC nor multiple GPU architectures.

4   Classifying Existing MPI GPU Triggering Proposals

In this section, we classify these proposals and their availablity or described implementations according to the taxonomy described in Sect. 3, as shown in Table 1. We then use this taxonomical classification to compare and contrast key features of these proposals and their corresponding implementations.

4.1   API Classification

We focus on the nine proposed GPU-triggered MPI programming interface extensions listed below:

MPI-GDS [17] – a GPU-triggering interface extension for the MVAPICH MPI implementation [16].

MCI-ACX Enqueued [1] – stream-triggered, two-sided communication operations as implemented in the MPI-ACX GPU-triggering interface extension for NVIDIA network devices that support MLX4 device functionality.

MPICH Triggering [18] – a GPU-triggering interface extension for the MPICH MPI implementation [7].

HPE Send/Recv [14] – a stream-triggered MPI interface extension for HPE systems with the Slingshot network interface [4].

Project Delorean [11] – a proposal for graph-based sequencing of MPI operations that including GPU triggering.

HPE One-sided [15] – a GPU-triggered Post/Start/Complete/Wait interface extension for HPE systems with the Slingshot network interface.

Partitioned Communication – the MPI partitioned communication API [12] supplemented with the `Pbuf_prepare` and partitioned collective operations recently proposed [8], and partially implemented by MPI-ACX [1].

HPE Persistent [5] – a kernel-triggered communication MPI interface extension for HPE systems with the Slingshot network interface [4].

Intel GPU-Initiated [9,10] – a GPU-initiated extension for Intel MPI[5].

Note that while multiple variants of some of these designs have been proposed in the MPI Forum Working groups, BOFs, and other venues, we focus on the above listed API descriptions and implementations as representative of the main existing approaches at the time of this publication.

4.2   API Feature Comparisons

Based on the comparison shown in Table 1, there is no clear agreement on whether stream or kernel triggering is preferable, either from an API, programmability/usability, implementation, or performance perspective. Most implementations seek to reuse portions of the API and maintain or strengthen the semantics of the API operations they use, and also separate initialization and initiation of API operations.

Almost every API allows the GPU to check for or wait for the completion of every MPI operation that they either initiate or start, enabling the GPU to avoid returning to the host execution context to ensure communication completion. The main exception is partitioned communication, where receives completion can be tested on the GPU using `Parrived`, but there is no equivalent call for testing for the completion of sends initiated from the kernel using `Pready` (the only available option is to check if all send partitions have completed using a single call to `Wait` or `Test` or one of their variants).

---

[5] Personal Communication, Dr. Daniel J. Holmes, Intel Corp., June 14, 2024.

Table 1. Taxonomy of MPI GPU-Triggered Communication Proposals

Proposal	Area 1 (Control Path Used)	Area 2: API Features (Reuses Existing APIs)	Changes API Semantics	Separate Initialize and Start	GPU Completion Support	Collective Support
MPI-GDS	Stream	Yes	Weaker	No	Full	Full[1]
MPI-ACX Enqueued	Stream	Yes[1]	No	Yes[1]	Full	No
MPICHTriggering	Stream	Yes	No[2]	No	Full	Partial
HPE Send-Recv	Stream	No	No	Yes	Full	No
Delorean	Stream	No[3]	No	Yes	Full	Full
HPE One-sided	Stream	Yes	Stronger[4]	Yes	Full	Group
Partitioned Comm.	Kernel	Yes	No	Yes	Partial[5]	Full[1]
HPE Persistent	Kernel	Yes	No	Yes	Full	No
Intel GPU-Init	Kernel	Yes	No	No	Full	No

Proposal	Area 3: Ordering and Concurrency (MPI Sequencing Object)	Sequencing Model Semantics	Concurrency Model Specified	Area 4: Implementation Considerations (GPU/NIC Progress)	Impl. Available	Multiple Arch. Support
MPI-GDS	No	N/A	Implicit	No	Yes	No
MPI-ACX Enqueued	No	N/A	No	No	Yes	NIC
MPICH Triggering	Yes	Full	Explicit	No	Yes	Yes
HPE Send/Recv	Yes	Partial	No	No	Yes	GPU
Delorean	Yes	Partial	Implicit	No	No	No
HPE One-sided	No	N/A	Implicit	Yes	Yes	GPU
Partitioned Comm.	No	N/A	Explicit	Yes	Yes	No
HPE Persistent	No	N/A	No	No	Yes	GPU
Intel GPU-Init	No	N/A	Yes	Yes	Yes	GPU

[1] Proposed in publication but not in the described or available implementations. [2] The initial proposal considered changing the semantics of `MPI_Send` and `MPI_Recv` on GPU stream communicators to be identical to their _enqueue variants and return to the caller prior to local completion of the operation; MPICH developers have since abandoned this approach. [3] Proposes "deferred" operations as a generalization of MPI persistent operations. [4] Explicitly defers `MPI_Put`/`MPI_Get` execution to when `MPI_Win_complete_stream` is called. [5] There is no GPU call to determine if a partition that has been marked ready to send has completed locally.

While several APIs propose collective support, only limited support for any GPU-triggered collectives is available, e.g., `MPIX_Allreduce_enqueue` in MPICH and point-to-point group communication in the HPE one-sided triggering API. This is likely due to the complexity of combining complex collective communication with the constrained GPU and NIC control paths.

There is little agreement on whether to introduce a new MPI-level primitive to represent GPU execution ordering, with some APIs introducing new primitives and others reusing opaque GPU streams. Note that this is the case even from the same vendor, where the HPE two-sided API includes an `MPI_Queue` object that is not used by the HPE one-sided API.

Implementation availability varies significantly. For instance, Delorean is just a specification with no known implementation; Intel's GPU support is currently in "preview," while MPI-ACX is fully available and so we were able to run the ping-ping example on representative hardware. Few implementations support full GPU/NIC offload of communication; most APIs designed with the assumption that the host will be involved in data movement.

5   Key Gaps

Based on the classifications described in the previous section, this section covers gaps and perceived limitations observed in prior work and prototypes as well as the MPI standard.

5.1   Limitations in the MPI Standard

In the MPI Standard, there are two main areas that needs to be addressed.

1. Problems surrounding persistence: The separation of initialization and starting in GPU triggering APIs make persistent operations attractive for this purpose, as demonstrated by partitioned communication. Unfortunately, MPI-1 specified persistent send and receive operations cannot communicate at initialization nor does their initialization result in matching; indeed, persistent and non-persistent operations can match each time they are started.
2. Lack of `MPI_Pbuf_prepare*` operations for two-sided communication: Two separate issues that have been conflated in prior discussions of `MPI_Pbuf-_prepare` and `MPI_Pbuf_prepareall`, yet to be standardized [6]:
   (a) Ensuring that MPI two-sided requests are matched (once and for all) so that there is agreement between the sender and receiver side about the exposed buffer on which to make operations (such as with `MPI_Puts` for early-bird communication as `MPI_Pready`'s are issued on the send side).
   (b) Ensuring or asserting that the remote buffer is *ready* for one-sided data movement; that is, there are no unexpected transfers.
   The former evidently subsumes the latter; otherwise, matching/synchronization would have to be done prior to every call to `MPI_Start`, which is likely to be unacceptably costly. Further, because of the allowance for weak progress in MPI implementations, there is no guarantee even in two-sided operations that match at initialization (e.g., in partitioned communication) that the initial match has occurred between before the first complete communication. Thus, initial communication can occur before any agreement on the readiness of the receive buffer (e.g., agreement and transmission could first transpire during the first wait calls, and/or the initial transfers could be orchestrated differently than subsequent ones).

In addition, the desire for these conditions is not unique to partitioned communication—the various stream-triggered communication proposals (MPICH, HPE two-sided, MPI-ACX enqueuing, etc.) would want this functionality to push their data movement through the one-sided path as well.

5.2   Limitations Across Proposed APIs

In addition to gaps in the MPI standard that increase the difficulty of supporting GPU triggering, there are also recurring limitations across the various APIs that have been proposed. We highlight these gaps below to encourage efforts to address them consistently in new and revised proposals:

- Clear concurrency model—If the host execution context and accelerator context both initiate or start operations, the ordering and concurrency is ill-defined in many APIs, are left to the vagueness of MPI, or are silent. MPICH stream triggering is the only one that provides a clear, specific concurrency model for both host- and accelerator-initiated communication.
- Matching—There is no explicit support for matching of send/receive buffers so that this occurs only once, and receive matching overheads are eliminated.
- GPU completion support with partitioning—If something is started on a GPU, there is no way to know if something is completed on the send side. This makes it difficult or impossible to write programs without need to synchronize with the CPU to interleave communication and computation.
- Collective communication support—This is broadly absent yet needed to support real applications that avoid unnecessary synchronization with the CPU. In particular, *no* current MPI stream triggering approach supports stream triggering of the full range of MPI collective communication operations.
- GPU/NIC Progress—Lack of this feature is a gap for any performant implementation. Out of the nine APIs considered only three (partitioned communication augmented with `Pbuf_prepare`, HPE one-sided communication, and Intel GPU-initiated) support GPU/NIC progress.

6   Conclusion

Message-passing communication involving GPUs with MPI has proven to be both complex and expensive, motivating new approaches. This is the first comprehensive survey of all nine proposals known to the authors that address stream/graph-, kernel-triggered, and GPU-initiated communication abstractions for MPI, whose principal purpose is to improve the performance of communication when GPU kernels create or consume data for transfer through MPI operations.

Here, we compared and contrasted stream/graph- and kernel-triggered MPI communication abstractions. Various proposals with distinct potential APIs for stream- and/or kernel-triggering have been proffered as designs and/or prototypes, which span various GPU architectures and approaches, including MPI-4 partitioned point-to-point communication, stream communicators, explicit MPI stream/queue objects, and notified-RMA. Notably, some of these proposals either strengthen or weaken the semantics of MPI operations. We enumerated nine different proposals and provided a taxonomy of these proposals and their operations against twelve categories of features and semantics.

We described the design space in which these abstractions reside, their use of stream and other non-MPI abstractions, their relationship to partitioned and persistent operations, and discussed their potential for added performance, how usable these are, and where functional and/or semantic gaps exist. Designs breaking backward compatibility with MPI were also duly noted (and cautioned). We also presented code examples of how some of these operate on the ubiquitous ping-pong use case (variously utilizing CUDA, ROCM, and Intel APIs).

The next steps to advance performance-portable programming with accelerator-based MPI+X programming should start with robust, inclusive conversations and design bake-offs among the various proposers, implementers, and users to identify a coherent path forward within the MPI community, inclusive of application developers. One or more proposed standard APIs would be competed then down-selected for MPI-5. Existing proposals/prototypes cited in this paper may not include all hardware vendors or systems currently available and certainly there may be other solutions forthcoming or that are not yet public (e.g., for FPGAs or other GPU accelerator products). Yet, fitting additional and/or forthcoming proposals, prototypes, and designs into our taxonomy will provide a coherent basis to compare and contrast these with the nine presented here.

Acknowledgments. The authors wish to acknowledge Dr. Daniel J. Holmes of Intel Corporation for providing information, examples, and references on the Intel GPU triggering API for this paper. The authors also wish to acknowledge Dr. Hui Zhou of Argonne National Laboratories for providing additional information and clarifications on the MPICH stream triggering API.

This work was performed with partial support from the National Science Foundation under Grants Nos. OAC-2103510, CCF-2405142 and CCF-2412182, the U.S. Department of Energy's National Nuclear Security Administration (NNSA) under the Predictive Science Academic Alliance Program (PSAAP-III), Award DE-NA0003966, and Tennessee Technological University. Any opinions, findings, and conclusions or recommendations expressed in this material are those of the authors and do not necessarily reflect the views of the National Science Foundation, or the U.S. Department of Energy's National Nuclear Security Administration.

Disclosure of Interests. The authors have no competing interests to declare that are relevant to the content of this article.

References

1. Dinan, J.: MPI-ACX: MPI Accelerator Extensions Prototype (2023). https://github.com/NVIDIA/mpi-acx
2. Dinan, J., et al.: Enabling communication concurrency through flexible MPI endpoints. Int. J. High Performance Comput. Appl.**28**(4), 390–405 (2014) 10.1177/1094342014548772, https://doi.org/10.1177/1094342014548772

3. Elis, B., Pearce, O., Böhme, D., Burmark, J., Schulz, M.: Non-blocking GPU-CPU notifications to enable more GPU-CPU parallelism. In: Proceedings of the International Conference on High Performance Computing in Asia-Pacific Region, HPCAsia 2024, Nagoya, Japan, January 25-27, 2024, pp. 1–11. ACM (2024). https://doi.org/10.1145/3635035.3635036

4. Enterprise, H.P.: HPE Slingshot Interconnect. https://www.hpe.com/in/en/compute/hpc/slingshot-interconnect.html

5. Enterprise, H.P.: MPIX_start - Cray MPICH Documentation (2024). https://cpe.ext.hpe.com/docs/mpt/mpich/mpix_start.html

6. Forum, M.: Synchronization on Partitioned Communication for Accelerator Optimization (2020). https://github.com/mpi-forum/mpi-issues/issues/302

7. Gropp, W.: MPICH2: a new start for MPI implementations. In: Kranzlmüller, D., Volkert, J., Kacsuk, P., Dongarra, J. (eds.) EuroPVM/MPI 2002. LNCS, vol. 2474, pp. 7–7. Springer, Heidelberg (2002). https://doi.org/10.1007/3-540-45825-5_5

8. Holmes, D.J., et al.: Partitioned collective communication. In: 2021 Workshop on Exascale MPI (ExaMPI), pp. 9–17. IEEE, St. Louis, MO, USA, Nov 2021). https://doi.org/10.1109/ExaMPI54564.2021.00007, https://ieeexplore.ieee.org/document/9652828/

9. Intel Corp.: Intel MPI Library Developer Reference for Linux, June 2024. https://www.intel.com/content/www/us/en/docs/mpi-library/developer-reference-linux/2021-12/overview.html

10. Intel Corp.: Intel MPI Library Developer Reference for Linux: GPU Buffers Support, June 2024. https://www.intel.com/content/www/us/en/docs/mpi-library/developer-reference-linux/2021-12/gpu-buffers-support.html#GUID-43A895E2-0FAC-4166-944C-67D5DE15A31C, This citation is for the Intel GPU-initiated interface and not the entire Intel MPI library

11. Koziol, Q.: Composable Asynchronous Communication Graphs and Streams in MPI (2023). https://github.com/mpiwg-hybrid/hybrid-issues/files/11680187/Project_Delorean-2023-06-07a.pdf

12. Message Passing Interface Forum: MPI: A Message-Passing Interface Standard Version 4.0, June 2021. https://www.mpi-forum.org/docs/mpi-4.0/mpi40-report.pdf

13. Message Passing Interface Forum: MPI: A Message-Passing Interface Standard Version 4.1, November 2023. https://www.mpi-forum.org/docs/mpi-4.1/mpi41-report.pdf

14. Namashivayam, N., Kandalla, K., White, T., Radcliffe, N., Kaplan, L., Pagel, M.: Exploring GPU Stream-Aware Message Passing using Triggered Operations, August 2022. http://arxiv.org/abs/2208.04817, arXiv:2208.04817 [cs]

15. Namashivayam, N., Kandalla, K., White III, J.B., Kaplan, L., Pagel, M.: Exploring Fully Offloaded GPU Stream-Aware Message Passing, June 2023. http://arxiv.org/abs/2306.15773, arXiv:2306.15773 [cs]

16. Panda, D.K., Subramoni, H., Chu, C.H., Bayatpour, M.: The MVAPICH project: Transforming research into high-performance MPI library for HPC community. J. Comput. Sci. **52**, 101208 (2021). https://doi.org/10.1016/j.jocs.2020.101208,https://www.sciencedirect.com/science/article/pii/S1877750320305093, case Studies in Translational Computer Science

17. Venkatesh, A., Hamidouche, K., Potluri, S., Rosetti, D., Chu, C.H., Panda, D.K.: MPI-GDS: high performance MPI designs with GPUDirect-aSync for CPU-GPU control flow decoupling. In: 2017 46th International Conference on Parallel Processing (ICPP), pp. 151–160. IEEE, Bristol, United Kingdom, August 2017. https:// doi.org/10.1109/ICPP.2017.24, http://ieeexplore.ieee.org/document/8025289/
18. Zhou, H., Raffenetti, K., Guo, Y., Thakur, R.: mpix stream: an explicit solution to hybrid MPI+X programming. In: Proceedings of the 29th European MPI Users' Group Meeting, pp. 1–10. ACM, Chattanooga TN USA, September 2022. https://doi.org/10.1145/3555819.3555820, https://dl.acm.org/doi/10.1145/3555819.3555820

Stream Support in MPI Without the Churn

Joseph Schuchart[1]([✉]) and Edgar Gabriel[2]

[1] Institute for Advanced Computational Science, Stony Brook University,
Stonybrook, NY, USA
`joseph.schuchart@stonybrook.edu`
[2] Advanced Micro Devices, Inc. (AMD), Austin, TX, USA

Abstract. Accelerators have become a corner stone of parallel computing, ranging from scientific computing to artificial intelligence. At the
application level, accelerators are controlled by submitting work into a
stream, from which the work is executed by the hardware. Vendor-specific
communication libraries such as NCCL and RCCL have integrated support for submitting communication operations onto a stream to enable
ordering of communication and work on streams. It is safe to assume that
stream-based computing will remain relevant for the foreseeable future.
MPI has yet to catch up to this reality and prior proposals involved
extensions of MPI that would incur significant additions to the API.

In this work, we explore alternatives that involve only minor additions to the standard to enable the integration of MPI operations with
compute stream. Our additions include i) associating streams with communication objects, ii) blocking streams until completion, and iii) synchronizing streams while progressing MPI operations. Our API is agnostic of the type of stream, reuses existing communication procedures and
semantics, and enables integration with graph capturing. We provide
a proof-of-concept implementation and show that stream integration of
MPI operations can be beneficial.

Keywords: accelerators · GPU · HIP · MPI · streams

1 Introduction

High-performance computing systems increasingly rely on compute accelerators
to solve the most complex and compute-intensive problems. Systems such as
the Frontier [16] and Summit [15] supercomputers achieve a majority of their
theoretical and practical compute performance from the GPU accelerators on
the compute nodes. These heterogeneous systems pose numerous challenges to
application developers. Accelerators often have separate memory with different performance characteristics than regular DRAM used by CPUs, which also
mandates different optimizations and (potentially) costly data transfers between
CPU and GPU memory. Furthermore, launching a compute kernel on an accelerator can incur significantly higher cost than invoking a function on the CPU.

C. Blaas-Schenner et al. (Eds.): EuroMPI 2024, LNCS 15267, pp. 56–72, 2025.
https://doi.org/10.1007/978-3-031-73370-3_4

Programming models for GPUs such as HIP [1], CUDA [14], or SYCL [2] are tailored towards dealing with these challenges. A primary goal of these programming models is to keep the GPUs busy and hide the costs of all associated operations, providing features such as asynchronous memory allocation and data transfers; the ability to express sequence of data transfers and compute operations in a logical order to allow for decoupling of the execution of GPU code from the CPU; or capturing a sequence of kernel operations as a graph to optimize the execution of the sequence in subsequent iterations.

One of the challenges facing application developers on these systems is the necessity to deal with two different programming models in a single code, such as using HIP for managing the compute operations within a node, and MPI [12] for managing communication between processes both within and across multiple nodes. MPI libraries such as Open MPI [6] and MPICH [7] have been supporting GPU devices for a number of years through a feature referred to as GPU-awareness. From a conceptual perspective, GPU-awareness only refers to an MPI library being able to send/receive data located in a GPU buffer, without necessarily making any statements on how the data transfer is implemented internally. In practice, MPI libraries have been able to achieve very good performance in scenarios where the platform supports peer-to-peer access between different GPUs for intra-node communication, and therefore exploit the very-high bandwidth between the GPUs often available such as the InfinityFabric^{TM} links between AMD GPUs. Similarly, most high-end network interconnects and their corresponding driver software support direct memory access (DMA) between the network interface card and the GPU memory, leading to similar device-to-device inter-node data transfer performance as with host memory.

Nevertheless, MPI has been lacking behind vendor-specific communication APIs regarding accelerator-based communication. For example, many GPU programming models support the concept of a *stream* as a commonly used abstraction for enqueuing GPU functions (kernels) for later execution. GPU kernels are subsequently executed in the same order as submitted to the stream, with kernel i having to wait for kernel $i-1$ to complete. Hence, streams allow to remove the CPU thread from the control flow of the application. MPI does not provide an infrastructure for applications to expose compute streams or to enqueue communication into compute streams. Instead, applications are required to wait for the completion of a stream (synchronize) before passing buffers affected by previous compute kernels on a stream to MPI.

Prior work has aimed at adding ways to enqueue communication into a stream [13, 22]. These proposals introduced new sets of functions that were specifically meant to enqueue communication. However, this would require a significant extension of MPI through duplication of functions. Moreover, these proposals were only concerned with enqueuing nonblocking operations into streams but neglected the interaction of blocking operations with streams.

In this work, we present what we believe is a minimal set of functions needed to integrate stream semantics with MPI. We rely on the blocking and nonblocking semantics of existing operations and require only minor additions to the standard to facilitate the interaction with streams.

2   Extension to MPI

We first provide an overview of our proposal to integrate MPI operations with compute streams, describe their semantics, and delve into the API extensions.

2.1   Overview

Our proposed extension to MPI consist of three parts: i) associating existing communication objects (communicators, files, and windows) with streams; ii) enqueuing communication synchronization points into streams; and iii) synchronizing streams while progressing MPI.

Our proposal follows two main goals: to maintain existing semantics of MPI operations and to avoid excessive additions to the MPI standard. The first point is important for usability since it helps users transition to using streams in MPI by not breaking with existing semantics. The second item ensures concise stream integration and avoids bloating the MPI standard in order to address changes in the compute environment.

By associating a stream to a communication object, the existing semantics for blocking, nonblocking, and partitioned communication operations are extended to the *execution context of the stream*. This is an important difference to today's semantics for blocking, nonblocking, and persistent operations, which apply only to the calling thread's execution context.

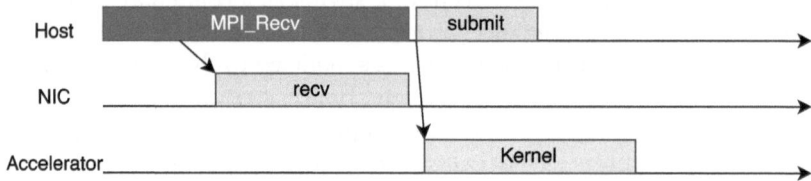

Fig. 1. MPI_Recv into a GPU buffer without an associated stream.

Blocking Operations. For example, a call to MPI_Recv without an associated stream will block the calling CPU thread until the message has been received and the data is available in the receive buffer, as shown in Fig. 1. This requires applications to synchronize the stream before calling the MPI communication procedure. In addition, if the subsequent GPU kernel uses the data buffer used in the MPI_Recv operation, launching the GPU kernel also has to be delayed until the completion of the MPI operation.

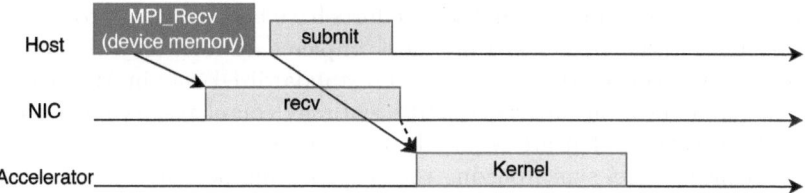

Fig. 2. MPI_Recv with an associated stream.

With a stream associated to a communicator, the calling thread may return before the operation is complete. The implementation must ensure that subsequent operations on the stream are deferred until the memory used in the operation is available, as shown in Fig. 2. In essence, the blocking semantics of the procedure call apply to the execution space of the associated stream to ensure consistency with subsequent operations. It is permissible but not required that the calling thread returns after the operation is complete. This provides implementations with flexibility on how to implement blocking communication procedures. A straight-forward implementation would be to synchronize the associated stream before initiating the communication operation. However, implementations may also offload the operation to the device and return from the procedure call before the operation is even started. Completion of the operation is assured once the next operation enqueued into stream is executed.

Nonblocking and Persistent Operations. Initiation of nonblocking operations and starting of persistent operations will remain local operations for the calling thread and do not block the execution of subsequent operations on the stream. Instead, the operation will be enqueued into the stream and will start once the stream reaches the respective position. A separate operation must be enqueued to block the stream until the operation is complete (Sect. 2.4). Subsequent operations on that stream will then be delayed until the memory can be safely accessed, e.g., data has been transferred out of a send buffer or deposited into a receive buffer. We believe that a function similar to MPI_Test would be of little use if applied to a stream and thus only provide an operation that blocks the stream. However, the application may still use MPI_Test or MPI_Wait on the nonblocking or persistent request to test for completion on the host or block the calling thread until completion.

In essence, the existence of an associated stream only defers the start of the operation until the stream has reached the respective position. It does not change the semantics of these operations. The use of nonblocking and persistent operations on a stream enables applications to post multiple operations on a stream, which helps avoid deadlocks that may occur in other models [18].

Stream Synchronization. One of the main sticking points of MPI is the issue of progress. While it has been argued that MPI implementations should provide strong progress guarantees [8] and some efforts have been made to provide strong progress [17, 21] the reality is that most implementations only provide weak progress guarantees. Currently there is no standardized way in MPI to ensure that all communication progresses and eventually completes, except for calling into MPI procedures that are required to ensure progress.

As a consequence, synchronizing the stream using non-MPI procedure calls after submitting kernels and MPI operations onto a stream may leave MPI without resources to ensure progress and thus block the stream indefinitely. It is beyond the scope of this paper to address the lack of strong progress guarantees in MPI in general, although having a standardized way of providing MPI with resources to ensure strong progress would alleviate this problem.

Instead, we propose adding a blocking procedure to MPI that ensures progress of MPI operations enqueued on the associated stream and returns after successful synchronization of the stream, i.e., once all operations on the stream have completed, including all pending communication operations.

2.2 Graph Capturing

The HIP API provides the concept of graphs, which allow a set of operations on a stream to be bundled and optimize the sequence of operations to minimize the cost of the kernel submissions. One way to create a graph is by capturing all operations that were submitted onto a stream and replaying the sequence of operations when the graph is executed. With our proposed extension, MPI operations can simply be integrated into a captured graph, avoiding breaks in the stream capturing due to communication operations.

2.3 Stream Management

The first step in our extension is to associate a stream with an MPI communication object. This allows MPI operations to synchronize with prior and subsequent operations on the stream.

Listing 1.1 lists the signatures of functions used to associate streams with communicators. While we only describe our API for communicators, we point out that similar procedures should be introduced for windows and files, which are left out here in the interest of brevity.

A call to `MPIX_Comm_set_stream` associates the stream with the communicator `comm`. The `kind` string parameter describes the kind of the stream. Examples currently included are `"hip"` and `"cuda"`. The `stream_ptr` argument is a pointer to the stream handle. This provides a generic interface that is agnostic to the underlying type of the stream handle object.

The `info` argument can be used in the future to extend the semantics of the association between the communicator and the stream. No info keys have been defined at this point.

```
1  int MPIX_Comm_set_stream(
2    MPI_Comm comm,
3    const char *kind, void *stream_ptr,
4    MPI_Info info, int *flag);
5
6  int MPIX_Comm_get_stream(
7    MPI_Comm, void *stream_ptr, int *flag);
8
9  int MPIX_Comm_delete_stream(MPI_Comm comm);
```

Listing 1.1. Stream management procedures for communicators.

Upon return, the `flag` output parameter will be set to `true` if the MPI implementation supports the given `kind`. Otherwise it will be set to `false`, indicating that the application must synchronize streams before invoking MPI communication procedures.

It is valid to associate a stream with a communicator that already has a stream associated. In that case, the new stream will be used for any subsequent operations issued on the communicator.

A call to `MPIX_Comm_get_stream` sets `flag` to `false` if no stream is associated with the communicator and `true` otherwise. In the latter case, the associated stream is returned in the variable pointed to by `stream_ptr`;

`MPIX_Comm_delete_stream` can be used to remove any associated stream from the given communicator. When replacing or deleting a stream, the implementation is not allowed to synchronize the stream and must be able to handle operations pending on the stream (e.g., through reference-counted meta-data).

2.4 Stream Wait Operations

Following existing semantics, nonblocking communication procedure calls will return immediately after enqueuing the operation onto the stream. The start of such operation will be deferred until the execution of the stream has reached the position at which the operation has been enqueued.

The resulting request object represents the operation and may still be used to test and wait for the operation to complete, using `MPI_Test` and `MPI_Wait` and their respective variants. However, the semantics of the test and wait calls will not change based on the fact that a stream had been associated with the communication object. This is a conscious choice and an important difference to blocking communication routines. This choice is motivated by the need for host-side facilities to test and wait for completion of operations without synchronizing the associated stream, even if the operation was associated with a stream. While a blocking operation associated with a stream is enqueued into the execution space of the stream (and the associated device), test and wait calls are executed in the host execution space.

```
1  int MPIX_Stream_wait(
2    MPI_Request *req,
3    MPI_Status *stat);
4
5  int MPIX_Stream_waitall(
6    int count,
7    MPI_Request reqs[],
8    MPI_Status stats[]);
```

Listing 1.2. Procedures to block associated streams until completion.

```
1  int MPIX_Comm_sync_stream(MPI_Comm comm);
```

Listing 1.3. Procedure to synchronize a stream associated with a communicator.

In order to facilitate completion of nonblocking operations as part of the stream execution, two new functions are introduced, as shown in Listing 1.2. A call to MPIX_Stream_wait will ensure that subsequent operations on the execution stream on which the MPI operation represented by req has been enqueued will be deferred until the operation completed. This effectively enqueues a wait operation into the stream. No subsequent operations enqueued on the stream after the wait operation may be executed before the result of the operation represented by req is available on the associated stream.

The behavior of MPIX_Stream_wait is similar to MPI_Wait in that the ownership of nonblocking operation requests is returned to MPI and the request handle is set to MPI_REQUEST_NULL. Contrary to MPI_Wait, however, MPIX_Stream_wait is a local procedure and does not wait for the operation to complete. Instead, the blocking nature of the wait applies to the execution space associated with the respective operation.

The status may be MPI_STATUS_IGNORE or a pointer to a status object that will be filled before the stream continues its execution past the completion of the operation. Both status objects and request handles must reside in host memory and are not required to be accessible on the device.

MPIX_Stream_waitall allows applications to enqueue multiple operation on a stream and complete them at once. The semantics of this procedure are similar to MPIX_Stream_wait with the addition that the stream is blocked until all count operations have completed. A call to MPIX_Stream_waitall is thus similar to count consecutive calls to MPIX_Stream_wait on each of the provided requests.

2.5 Stream Synchronization

Listing 1.3 lists the signature of MPIX_Comm_sync_stream, which progresses outstanding MPI operations and returns only once all operations on the stream

```
 1  int flag, bytes=SIZE*sizeof(int), *buf; // device buffer
 2  int copydir = cudaMemcpyDeviceToHost;
 3  MPI_Comm comm = MPI_COMM_WORLD;
 4  hipStream_t stream;
 5  hipStreamCreateWithFlags(&stream, hipStreamNonBlocking);
 6  // set the stream and check for success
 7  MPIX_Comm_set_stream(comm, "hip", &flag, &stream);
 8  if (!flag) MPI_Abort(comm, ENOSYS);
 9  // allocate GPU device memory
10  hipMallocAsync((void**)&buf, bytes, stream);
11  // submit compute kernel
12  compute<<<..., stream>>>(buf, SIZE);
13  // send GPU buffer to peer progress
14  MPI_Isend(buf, SIZE, MPI_INT, peer, tag, comm, &req);
15  // copy device buffer to host
16  hipMemcpyAsync(host_buf, buf, bytes, copydir, stream);
17  // enqueue wait for send
18  MPIX_Stream_wait(&req, MPI_STATUS_IGNORE);
19  // free the device buffer
20  hipFreeAsync(buf, stream);
21  // synchronize stream: wait for operations to complete
22  MPIX_Comm_sync_stream(comm);
```

Listing 1.4. Example using a communicator with an associated HIP stream.

associated with `comm` have completed. In essence, this function subsumes the functionality of `hipStreamSynchronize`, which if called by itself on a stream with pending MPI operations may be insufficient and cause deadlocks due to the lack of progress in MPI. Thus, this procedure provides applications with a way to ensure progress in MPI while waiting for a stream. MPI implementations already integrate device programming models such as HIP so it appears natural to move the synchronization of streams into MPI to ensure mutual progress.

2.6   Example Use Case

Listing 1.4 shows an example of how a nonblocking send operation can be integrated within a program using stream-based memory allocation and data movement operations in the HIP programming model. After associating the communicator with a stream and checking for support from the implementation (Lines 7–8), the example enqueues both memory allocation and a kernel onto the stream. The subsequent call to `MPI_Isend` (Line 14) will enqueue the start of the operation to occur after the completion of the `compute` kernel. The interaction of the nonblocking send operation with the stream avoids an otherwise necessary stream synchronization before the call to `MPI_Isend`.

The separation of initiation and completion of the nonblocking send operation on the stream (Lines 14–18) allows for potential overlap of the send with the asynchronous memory movement operation (Line 16) but will ensure that the send has completed before the asynchronous memory release (Line 20).

Due to space constraints we omit presenting an example for graph capturing using the syntax proposed in this paper. The repository containing the prototype implementation presented in the next section contains however an example demonstrating this scenario.

3 Implementation

We implemented a proof-of-concept (PoC) to demonstrate the feasibility of this approach.[1] Our implementation is based on the HIP programming model and thus can easily be adapted to CUDA. We are confident that our approach could be adapted to other device programming models with stream semantics. Our implementation is available as a stand-alone library that intercepts some of the existing MPI function calls using the PMPI library interposition interface and utilize the MPI Continuations functionality [20] to react to the completion of operations. The PoC is currently limited to nonblocking and persistent send and receive operations. However, we believe that this does not limit the generality of our approach.

3.1 Stream-Based Operations

In our implementation, streams are bound to communicators through an attribute on the communicator. This allows us to query the associated stream any time the communicator is passed into a communication functions.

Once we encounter a communication call on a communicator with an associated stream, the operation is enqueued into the stream using one of two ways: using the host-side callback API or the event API. The first method enqueues a callback using `hipLaunchHostFunc`, which is invoked once all prior operations on the stream have completed.

Unfortunately, callback functions are not reentrant, i.e., calls into the HIP API from within host-side callbacks are not allowed. A direct call to MPI procedures within the host-side function callback may lead to HIP function calls inside the MPI implementation, which is agnostic to its call-site. Thus, the host-side callback has to create a work descriptor that is pushed into a queue from which it is executed by a thread outside of the host-side callback. For nonblocking operations, this work descriptor initiates the operation (e.g., by calling `MPI_Isend`). For persistent operations, on the other hand, the work item simply consists of starting the operation (i.e., calling `MPI_Start` on the relevant request).

If the event API is used instead, an event is recorded (using `hipEventRecord`) and inserted into a list of active events with its respective operation. As part

---

[1] Our PoC is available at https://github.com/devreal/mpix-streams-pub.

of the progress loop (i.e., in `MPIX_Comm_sync_stream`), active events are queried for completion (using `hipEventQuery`), and if found complete the associated operation is started. We cache inactive events to mitigate the cost of event creation and destruction.

For nonblocking operations, our implementation returns a generalized request since the actual operation has not been started yet. In the absence of attributes on requests, we track the association between these requests and the operation descriptor in a separate data structure.

We acknowledge that there may be more efficient implementations, e.g., using device-triggered operations [13, 18]. However, the focus of this work was on the design of the extension to the MPI standard.

3.2   Stream-Based Wait

A call to `MPIX_Stream_wait` ensures that the stream does not progress past the current position unless the respective operation is complete. To achieve this, we utilize the signal memory API available in HIP to block and release the stream (`hipStreamWaitValue64` and `hipStreamWriteValue64`). Each subsequent MPI operation for which a wait is enqueued on the stream is assigned a monotonically increasing identifier. Inside the call to `MPIX_Stream_wait`, the stream is set up to wait for the next identifier is released.

A continuation is attached to the communication operation, in which the respective identifier is written to the signal memory to release the stream. Since MPI operations are not guaranteed to complete in the order in which they were started (e.g., a stream-based receive may complete before a send operation earlier in the stream) we ensure that the stream is not released prematurely and that the monotonic order of values waited on is adhered to.

Based on the implementation of nonblocking operations and stream-wait, we can implement blocking MPI operations as a combination of their nonblocking equivalent and `MPIX_Stream_wait`.

3.3   Graph Capturing

A HIP application can be set into a mode where operations on the stream are recorded but not executed. This stream of operations is captured into a graph that subsequently can be submitted multiple times. This allows the runtime systems to apply optimizations to the graph (e.g., by aggregating subsequent kernel submissions). We have thus explored ways for MPI to support graph capturing, i.e., to insert MPI operations into a captured graph.

The same mechanisms used for stream-integration can be used for graph capturing. However, some subtle differences have to be taken into account. Most importantly, the operations must be set up to be recurrent, i.e., it must be able to be started more than once. This is contrary to the simple stream integration, where the resources associated with a stream-based operation (e.g., the descriptor used in the host-side callback) can be released once the operation has been started. Instead, the resources acquired during stream-capture must be retained until the stream is removed from the communication object, e.g., through a call to `MPIX_Comm_delete_stream`.

Moreover, any activity not already implicitly captured by the stream must be integrated into the stream. For example, the continuation callback registration, which in the simple stream integration can be executed directly inside the call to `MPIX_Stream_wait`, must be triggered through a host-side callback. Although not explicitly stated, it appears that events cannot be used to detect stream progression, thus the usage of the event API for starting operations is not available.

3.4 Progress Considerations

The OpenCL [10] standard provides details on blocking and nonblocking behavior of function calls. Unfortunately, the documentation for HIP and CUDA do not define for all function calls whether they are guaranteed to be synchronous. Thus, a thread submitting kernels and MPI operations onto a stream may block in one of the HIP function calls. While strong guarantees on asynchronous behavior are desirable, we acknowledge that fact that enqueuing MPI operation *may* lead to deadlocks due to a lack in progress of MPI operations blocking a stream, i.e., because the calling thread does not reach into `MPIX_Comm_sync_stream`. We thus provide an optional implementation of strong progress (enabled through the environment variable `MPIX_STREAM_PROGRESS`). Usage of this facility incurs additional overhead (as observed in [13]) but may be useful for debugging, although we have not encountered a need for it.

4 Evaluation

We have evaluated our implementation on a single node of Frontier, hosted at Oak Ridge National Laboratory [16]. Each node has one 64-core AMD EPYC^{TM} 7A53 CPU and four AMD Instinct^{TM} MI250X, with each MI250X having two Graphics Compute Dies (GDC). We used one GCD per process. All our codes were compiled using Clang 15.0. The Open MPI implementation with support for MPI Continuations[2] was based on Open MPI's main branch at git hash `9656f59`. We used ROCm version 6.0 in our tests.

For the evaluation, we constructed a benchmark that consists of one kernel with a configurable runtime, followed by a communication operation (either nonblocking send or receive) and a second submission of the first kernel. We model the communication operation to be dependent upon the completion of the first kernel but independent of (and concurrently with) with the second kernel. Each iteration inside the kernel reads 64M `double` elements (512 MB). The number of iterations is configurable, allowing us to adjust the total runtime of the kernel.

---

[2] Available at https://github.com/devreal/ompi/tree/mpi-continue-master.

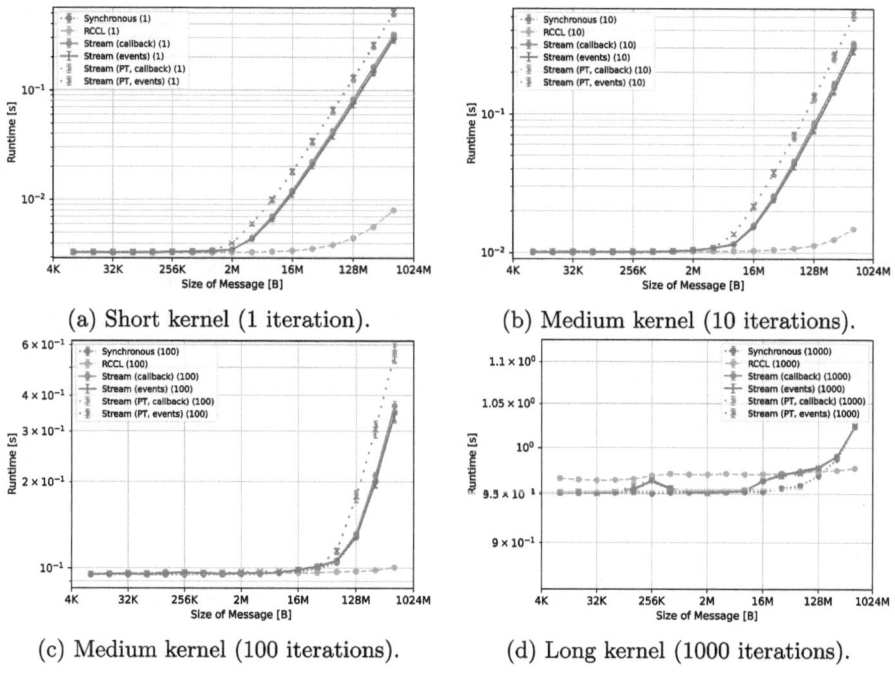

(a) Short kernel (1 iteration).

(b) Medium kernel (10 iterations).

(c) Medium kernel (100 iterations).

(d) Long kernel (1000 iterations).

Fig. 3. Runtime of different implementations under varying kernel runtimes.

We compare five variations of this setup using MPI. In the `Synchronous` variant the MPI communicator has no stream attached and the benchmark synchronizes the stream after the first kernel invocation, before calling `MPI_Isend`, before the second kernel submission, and `MPI_Wait` before waiting for the second kernel to complete. The `Stream` variants represent the configurations discussed above: the stream is associated with the communicator and the send/receive operations are enqueued into the stream using `MPI_Isend` and `MPI_Irecv`. We enqueue a wait operation using `MPIX_Stream_wait` after the second kernel submission and wait for completion using `MPIX_Comm_sync_stream`. Each variant used either events or callbacks and the ones marked with `PT` employ a background thread.

We also include a similar setup using the ROCm Communication Collectives Library (RCCL)[3] instead of MPI, in which we enqueue send and receive operations into the stream. RCCL differs from our MPI setup in that the communication is blocking on the stream, i.e., the second kernel does not execute before the communication operation has completed.

We measured at least 8 repetitions of the benchmark, each repetition reporting the mean of 10 iterations. Both the mean and standard deviation of the 8 repetitions are shown. Figure 3 shows the runtime of the benchmark using differ-

---

[3] https://github.com/ROCm/rccl.

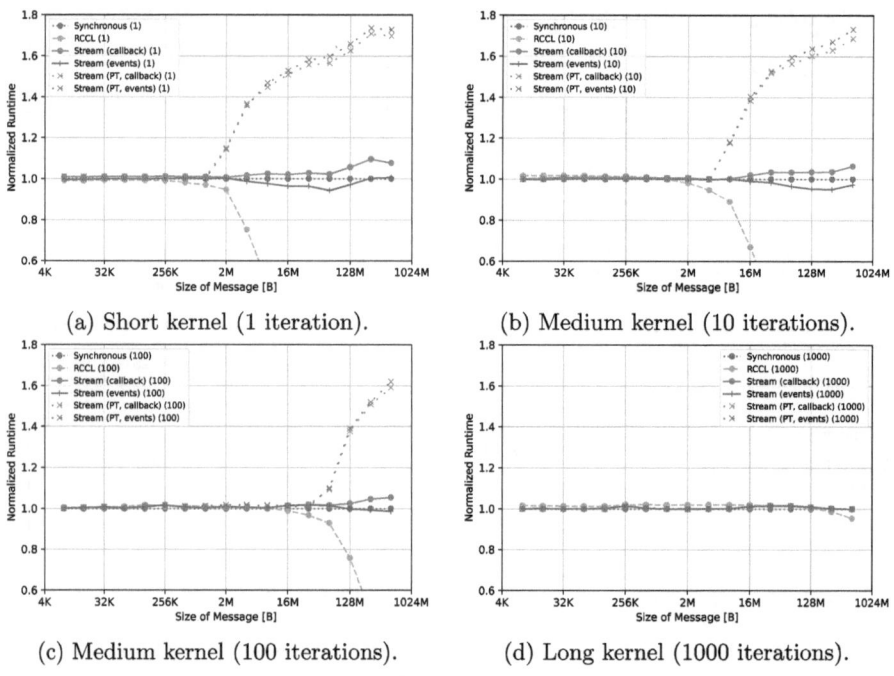

(a) Short kernel (1 iteration).   (b) Medium kernel (10 iterations).

(c) Medium kernel (100 iterations).   (d) Long kernel (1000 iterations).

Fig. 4. Normalized runtime of different implementations.

ent implementations and four different kernel runtimes. For small and medium size kernels (Fig. 3a–c), the biggest differences can be observed for messages above 2 MB: the variants using a progress thread yield the highest latency while RCCL yields the lowest latency, by up to one order of magnitude. For the longest running kernel (1000 iterations, Fig. 3d) we find that MPI yields lower runtimes for small and medium size messages over RCCL. This indicates that MPI is able to overlap the communication with the kernel execution in these cases while with RCCL the stream is blocked until the communication is complete.

Figure 4 presents the above data normalized to the Synchronous variant to provide a closer look at the differences. The data suggests that the progress thread introduces significant overheads, especially for larger messages and shorter kernel runtimes. However, we find that the stream integration itself yields mixed results, showing slight speedups for larger messages, if events are used instead of callbacks. We defer to prior work for a demonstration of the benefits of stream integration for device-triggered communication [13].

5   Discussion

The proposed API constitutes what we believe is a minimum extension to MPI to achieve stream integration of MPI communication operations. It is an attempt to integrate blocking, nonblocking, persistent, and partitioned operation semantics into the execution space of compute streams. We believe that the execution space is a separate dimension from the type of operation and that there are use-cases for all four types in the context of compute streams. Moreover, MPI communication objects such as communicators carry all the information needed to provide the MPI communication semantics. It thus seems natural to associate execution space information with such an object.

We acknowledge that the API, as proposed, does have short-comings. For example, multiple threads communicating on the same communicator but with different streams is currently not supported. We believe that allowing thread-specific association of streams would be a feasible option to address this.

We also note that the association of a stream implies changes to the semantics of blocking procedures for the calling host thread. The authors of [22] argue that these subtle differences are not obvious and thus reject implicit stream semantics. It should be noted, however, that there is precedence for diverging semantics in the form of the `"mpi_assert_allow_overtaking"` info key, which disables strict ordering of messages [19], and that the semantics of the communicator are controlled by the application and part of the contract between the application and libraries that may not be aware of such changes.

The comparison with RCCL shows that stream-integration is itself not sufficient to achieve significant performance improvements. Compared to MPI, the semantics of RCCL (and similar libraries) is significantly simpler, with a lack of tags, derived datatypes, and wildcards. This allows the message handling in RCCL to be fully offloaded to the device, minimizing synchronization with and involvement of the host CPU.

Past work in MPI has leveraged a host-side progress thread to fulfill the MPI message matching semantics [13]. In the future, however, offloading the message queue of a communicator with an associated stream to the respective device could be a viable pathway toward matching the performance of RCCL. It is likely that additional constraints will be needed, including guarantees that both peers communicate on communicators with associated streams as well as the already existing guarantees that no wildcards will be used.

While we consider device integration to be an important stepping stone to achieving similar performance by enabling stream-ordered communication, it is also important to note that stream integration in MPI is not only important for performance but plays a vital role in ensuring correctness. With streams associated to communication objects, applications are no longer required to explicitly synchronize streams before communicating device-side buffers, which has been a source of programming errors in the past.

6   Related Work

Zhou et al. [22] introduce the abstraction of an `MPIX_Stream`, which represents a serial execution context that could be mapped either to a Stream within a GPU programming model (e.g., `hipStream_t`), but also allows to define similar mechanism for regular CPU memory using e.g., OpenMP. Conceptually, each MPIX_Stream could/should be associated with a separate endpoint in the MPI library, hence allowing each stream to utilize different network resources. The MPIX_Stream can subsequently be used to create a communicator with stream association (MPIX_Stream_comm_create). The application can enqueue communication operations using a new set of API functions which take the stream-enhanced communicator as argument (e.g., MPIX_Send_enqueue). While the approach has some similarities to the one presented in this paper, the major difference lies in [22] introducing new enqueue functions for the actual communication operations, which would significantly increase the total number of APIs in the MPI specification. The API proposed by Zhou *et al.* also lacks important details such as MPIX_Comm_sync_stream used to ensure MPI progress while synchronizing a stream.

Namashivayam *et al.* introduce stream-triggered communication operations [13]. The core of the proposal is a new MPIX_Queue object that allows to enqueue communication operations using a new set of API functions (e.g., MPIX_Enqueue_send). A key difference to the previous project is the notion of *starting* the enqueued operations on a queue object (MPIX_Enqueue_start). This approach reduces the synchronization costs between a GPU kernel in a stream and subsequent pending communication operations by initiating (potentially) multiple communication operations simultaneously. Since an MPIX_Queue is, however, not directly associated with for example a hipStream_t, the suggested API would not allow to seamlessly integrate with stream-capture semantics discussed in this paper.

The question of how stream semantics can be integrated into the MPI standard has been an ongoing topic in the MPI Hybrid & Accelerator working group [5]. The works cited above are part of that effort. The API laid out in this contribution is an incarnation of an idea mentioned there [5].

The NVIDIA Collective Communication Library (NCCL [9]) provides an API that directly incorporates CUDA streams as arguments to communication routines. The extensions proposed in this paper, in contrast, attempt to integrate stream semantics into an API that was conceived over a decade before the concept of GPU programming was introduced [4,11]. Prior work has, however, evaluated the integration of NCCL in MPI applications [3].

7   Conclusions

We have proposed an extension to the MPI standard that associates compute streams with MPI communication objects to facilitate ordering of communication operations with kernel execution. We described our design to integrate blocking, nonblocking, and persistent operations with compute streams and how the proposed interface can be used in a captured graph, which has not been considered before. Contrary to previous proposals, our approach aims at minimizing the number of new functions that have to be introduced into the MPI standard and we believe that the execution context of an operation is an property separate from the semantics of the operation. We thus extend existing semantics to the execution context of streams and employ existing communication procedures to start operations. We only added functionality for associating streams with communication objects, for blocking the execution of streams until nonblocking and persistent operations have completed, and for waiting for a stream to complete while ensuring MPI progress.

We discussed different possible implementations (using either host-side callbacks or events) and showed that with sufficiently large kernel runtimes the stream integration can be beneficial. Additional research will be necessary to improve the efficiency of implementations and to explore the integration of additional features of stream-based execution models, including explicit graph construction. We also think that a benchmark reflecting real-world use-cases for stream-integrated communication is needed to evaluate research in this direction and to demonstrate performance impacts.

Acknowledgements. This research was supported partly by NSF awards #1931384 and #1931387. This research used resources of the Oak Ridge Leadership Computing Facility at the Oak Ridge National Laboratory, which is supported by the Office of Science of the U.S. Department of Energy under Contract No. DE-AC05-00OR22725.

References

1. Advanced Micro Devices, Inc.: HIP documentation (2024). https://rocm.docs.amd.com/projects/HIP/en/latest/index.html
2. Alpay, A., Heuveline, V.: SYCL beyond OpenCL: the architecture, current state and future direction of hipSYCL. In: Proceedings of the International Workshop on OpenCL, p. 1 (2020)
3. Awan, A.A., Manian, K.V., Chu, C.H., Subramoni, H., Panda, D.K.: Optimized large-message broadcast for deep learning workloads: MPI, MPI+NCCL, or NCCL2? Parallel Comput. (C) (2019). https://doi.org/10.1016/j.parco.2019.03.005
4. Bolz, J., Farmer, I., Grinspun, E., Schröder, P.: Sparse matrix solvers on the GPU: conjugate gradients and multigrid. ACM Trans. Graph. (TOG) **22**(3), 917–924 (2003). https://doi.org/10.1145/882262.882364
5. Dinan, J.: MPI Hybrid & Accelerator (HACC) WG Kickoff, December 2020. https://github.com/mpiwg-hybrid/hybrid-issues/blob/master/slides/2020-12-02%20--%20WG%20Kickoff%20(Jim%20Dinan).pdf
6. Gabriel, E., et al.: Open MPI: goals, concept, and design of a next generation MPI implementation. In: Proceedings. 11th European PVM/MPI Users' Group Meeting, Budapest, Hungary, pp. 97–104, September 2004
7. Gropp, W., Lusk, E., Doss, N., Skjellum, A.: A high-performance, portable implementation of the MPI message passing interface standard. Parallel Comput. **22**(6), 789–828 (1996)
8. Holmes, D.J., Skjellum, A., Schafer, D.: Why is MPI (perceived to be) so complex? Part 1-does strong progress simplify MPI? In: Proceedings of the 27th European MPI Users' Group Meeting, EuroMPI/USA 2020, pp. 21–30. Association for Computing Machinery (2020). https://doi.org/10.1145/3416315.3416318
9. Jeaugey, S.: Nccl 2.0. In: GPU Technology Conference (GTC), vol. 2, p. 23 (2017)

10. Khronos OpenCL Working Group: The opencl specification, April 2024. https:// registry.khronos.org/OpenCL/specs/3.0-unified/html/OpenCL_API.html
11. Krüger, J., Westermann, R.: Linear algebra operators for GPU implementation of numerical algorithms. ACM Trans. Graph. **22**(3), 908–916 (2003). https://doi.org/ 10.1145/882262.882363
12. Message Passing Interface Forum: MPI: A Message-Passing Interface Standard Version 4.1, November 2023. https://www.mpi-forum.org/docs/mpi-4.1/mpi41-report.pdf
13. Namashivayam, N., Kandalla, K., White, T., Radcliffe, N., Kaplan, L., Pagel, M.: Exploring GPU stream-aware message passing using triggered operations. arXiv preprint arXiv:2208.04817 (2022)
14. NVIDIA: The CUDA Zone (2009). http://www.nvidia.com/cuda
15. ORNL: Summit – Americas newest and smartest supercomputer (2018). https:// www.olcf.ornl.gov/summit/
16. ORNL: Frontier – ORNL's exascale supercomputer is delivering world-leading performance in 2022 and beyond (2022). https://www.olcf.ornl.gov/frontier/
17. Ouyang, K., Si, M., Hori, A., Chen, Z., Balaji, P.: Daps: a dynamic asynchronous progress stealing model for MPI communication. In: 2021 IEEE International Conference on Cluster Computing (CLUSTER), pp. 516–527 (2021). https://doi.org/ 10.1109/Cluster48925.2021.00027
18. Pan, L., Liu, J., Yuan, J., Zhang, R., Li, P., Xiao, Z.: OCCL: a deadlock-free Library for GPU collective communication (2023)
19. Patinyasakdikul, T., Eberius, D., Bosilca, G., Hjelm, N.: Give MPI threading a fair chance: a study of multithreaded MPI designs. In: 2019 IEEE International Conference on Cluster Computing (CLUSTER) (2019). https://doi.org/10.1109/ CLUSTER.2019.8891015
20. Schuchart, J., Samfass, P., Niethammer, C., Gracia, J., Bosilca, G.: Callback-based completion notification using MPI continuations. Parallel Comput. **106**, 102793 (2021). https://doi.org/10.1016/j.parco.2021.102793
21. Si, M., Peña, A.J., Hammond, J., Balaji, P., Takagi, M., Ishikawa, Y.: Casper: an asynchronous progress model for MPI RMA on many-core architectures. In: 2015 IEEE International Parallel and Distributed Processing Symposium, pp. 665–676 (2015). https://doi.org/10.1109/IPDPS.2015.35
22. Zhou, H., Raffenetti, K., Guo, Y., Thakur, R.: MPIX stream: an explicit solution to hybrid MPI+X programming. In: Proceedings of the 29th European MPI Users' Group Meeting, EuroMPI/USA 2022, pp. 1–10. Association for Computing Machinery, New York, NY, USA (2022). https://doi.org/10.1145/3555819.3555820

Improvements for MPI

Improved MPI Collectives for 3D-FFT

Yuang Yan$^{(\boxtimes)}$, Natasha Kuk, and Ryan E. Grant

Electrical and Computer Engineering Department, Queen's University,
11 Union Street, Kingston, ON, Canada
{yuang.yan,natasha.kuk,ryan.grant}@queensu.ca

Abstract. 3-dimensional Fast Fourier Transform (3D FFT) parallel computations are an important part of many scientific calculations. For example, 3D FFT is a critical component of molecular dynamics codes when they compute long range electrostatic computations. Parallel distributed 3D FFT computations involve redistributing intermediate data, which constitutes a substantial portion of overall execution time of these operations. There are two primary methods for handling this communication phase: explicitly packing and unpacking data, or using Message Passing Interface (MPI) derived datatypes. Derived datatypes have several advantages in that they are easy to work with and don't require explicit memory pack and unpack operations. As such we propose enhancements for derived datatypes in MPI specifically for 3D FFT calculations which improves upon state of the art methods [8] by using `MPI_Type_create_subarray` to support arbitrary storage orders. Our method reduces the performance issues associated with MPI derived datatype solutions and benefits from avoiding strided-memory operations in FFT execution. Results show that we can speedup even strong scaled 3DFFT by 1.17X to 1.44X using our method over previous state of the art methods.

1 Introduction

The Discrete Fourier Transform (DFT) is a fundamental tool in digital signal processing, converting discrete data from the time domain to the frequency domain. 1D and 2D DFTs are applied in processing audio and image signals while 3D DFT is applied in physical problems such as MRI image reconstruction [18] and molecular dynamics simulations [14]. The Fast Fourier Transform (FFT) is an efficient algorithm for computing 1D DFTs, reducing time complexity from $O(N^2)$ to $O(NlogN)$ [6].

Leveraging the separability property of DFT, multi-dimensional DFTs can be computed through a series of lower-dimensional FFTs for each dimension regardless of the order of transform, enabling parallelization of 3D DFT computations. One of the parallelization techniques is called *slab decomposition*. Here, the 3D array is split along a certain axis with processors executing independent 2D FFTs before the data is redistributed along another axis to complete the remaining FFT on the first distributed axis. Given the intense computation complexity

© The Author(s), under exclusive license to Springer Nature Switzerland AG 2025
C. Blaas-Schenner et al. (Eds.): EuroMPI 2024, LNCS 15267, pp. 75–88, 2025.
https://doi.org/10.1007/978-3-031-73370-3_5

and data size, performing 3D FFTs on clusters with MPI is common practice. In this process, the communication overhead of processors swapping intermediate results and managing the local memory layout contributes to most of the execution time of the FFT. The 3D array is distributed along 2 axes in this process, the local array is therefore divided into chucks departing for different ranks of processes. Elements in those truncated chunks are non-contiguous in the memory, leading to inefficiency in accessing the data as contiguous memory interactions are the easiest for computing hardware to understand and attempt to help in speeding up memory access through pre-fetching and being efficient with gathering only relevant data (as opposed to portions or relevant data) from each memory access.

To deal with non-contiguous data redistribution, one approach is to use MPI derived data types (DDT) to pack data and with MPI communication routines. Chatterjee et al. used `MPI_Type_vector` with `MPI_Isend/Irecv` [5] while Dalcin et al. proposed a concise method using `MPI_Type_create_subarray` with `MPI_Alltoallw` [8]. Both methods use identical DDT storage order on the sending and receiving side. While no explicit global transpose happens in those methods, they require strided FFT computation in the subsequent computation. This leads to unideal use of memory access as we will show in Sect. 6. An alternative method devised by Hoefler et al. in performing 2D FFT is to use different DDT storage orders on the sending and receiving side, eliminating the need for strided FFT in the last step [12]. However, we found that communication performance degrades when using different DDTs, and under some circumstances, the time gained by contiguous FFT can be easily offset by a longer communication time. This phenomenon has not yet been studied in previous works.

In this paper, we make the following contributions:

– We improve upon previous methods [8] by extending the functionalities of `MPI_Type_create_subarray` with support of arbitrary memory storage order description, including unconventional storage orders other than row-major or column-major order. By using the extended data type implementation, we avoided strided data accessing in FFT computation.
– We evaluate the impact of using different DDT in MPI collective communication, and managed to mitigate the performance issues by selecting appropriate sending/receiving storage orders of datatypes.

2   Background

In the MPI standard, derived datatypes are constructed using various type constructors. For instance, users can provide parameters such as strides and block lengths to the `MPI_Type_vector` to create arrays with evenly spaced elements. These derived datatypes can also be constructed recursively to handle more complex memory layouts, known as *typemaps*. Once a derived datatype is created, the MPI library manages the packing and unpacking of data, relieving programmers from the need to manually handle these tasks for each communication. Because of its simplicity, MPI derived datatypes are extensively utilized in scientific computing applications.

In the case of computation involving matrices, it is often necessary to perform operations using shared data or rearranging data elements for a single operation. MPI contains many such collective operations. One useful example is alltoall, which can be used to redistribute data, such as in a matrix transposition. `MPI_Alltoallw` is an advanced interface for this operation, which allows for variable datatypes and number of elements, making it suitable for scenarios where the data could not be evenly partitioned over the processes.

While MPI Collectives are often more time-efficient than manually exchanging elements one-by-one, they still constitute significant communication time. A single collective operation will still often take as long as multiple point-to-point communications, as typically not every exchange can happen simultaneously.

3   Proposed Method

A key element in improving the performance of 3D FFTs is memory access patterns. The arrangement of data in memory matters for performance. For example, when reading 8 8-byte double values in C, if they are in contiguous memory and aligned to cache lines, all 64 bytes of data can be read in a single operation (cache line). If they are distributed in memory, it could be necessary to perform up to 8 separate memory operations to fetch the same data. In our proposed method we strive to always provide the data needed for the current phase of the 3D FFT solve in contiguous memory, providing excellent memory efficiency for computation. We also wish to provide flexibility in how the data is arranged in memory and support 3D FFTs of different shapes, beyond typical cubic approaches. In order to achieve this, we propose new MPI functionality.

3.1   Extended MPI Subarray with Arbitrary Storage Order

```
int MPI_Type_create_subarray(int ndims, const int array_of_sizes[],
const int array_of_subsizes[], const int array_of_starts[],
int order, MPI_Datatype oldtype, MPI_Datatype *newtype)
```

The `MPI_Type_create_subarray` function, as defined, enables the creation of subarray datatypes with specified dimensions and storage orders. Traditionally, this function supported only row-major (`MPI_ORDER_C`) and column-major (`MPI_ORDER_FORTRAN`) storage orders. In our extended version, we allow for the specification of any shuffled storage order using an integer array of dimension lengths. The revised prototype of `MPIX_Type_create_subarray_x` is as follows:

```
int MPIX_Type_create_subarray_x(int ndims, const int array_of_sizes[],
const int array_of_subsizes[], const int array_of_starts[],
const int order[], MPI_Datatype oldtype, MPI_Datatype *newtype)
```

We use a $3 \times 3 \times 3$ indexed cubic array to illustrate the use of the vectorized order argument. Order $(0, 1, 2)$ refers to the conventional row-major order where elements are stored sequentially along the x, y, and z axes. We mark those elements with a series of consecutive numbers $\{0, 1, 2, 3, \ldots, 27\}$ in row-major order. Similarly, conventional column-major order is represented by $(2, 1, 0)$, and elements are stored along the z, y, and x axes. The memory layout of order $(2, 1, 0)$ is as follows:

0, 9, 18, 3, 12, 21, 6, 15, 24, 1, 10, 19, 4, 13, 22, 7, 16, 25, 2, 11, 20, 5, 14, 23, 8, 17, 26

By extending support to unconventional storage orders like $(2, 0, 1)$, where the z-axis is prioritized followed by x and y, we achieve alternative memory layouts. The memory layout will be as follows:

0, 9, 18, 1, 10, 19, 2, 11, 20, 3, 12, 21, 4, 13, 22, 5, 14, 23, 6, 15, 24, 7, 16, 25, 8, 17, 26

Our revised method provides more flexibility in subarray storage orders. We will show the benefits of using unconventional storage orders in optimizing the communication of redistribution time in Sect. 5.2.

3.2 Development

We adopt a recursive approach to construct N-dimensional ordered subarrays by nesting MPI vector datatypes. Given a set of assembled n-dimensional subarrays, denoted as A, where $A = \{A_{i_1, i_2, \ldots, i_n} \mid 1 \le i_1 \le l_1, 1 \le i_2 \le l_2, \ldots, 1 \le i_n \le l_n\}$ used to generate a $n + 1$ dimensional subarray A', where $A' = \{A'_{i_1, i_2, \ldots, i_{n+1}} \mid 1 \le i_1 \le l_1, 1 \le i_2 \le l_2, \ldots, 1 \le i_{n+1} \le l_{n+1}\}$. The axis length of the original array and subarray is denoted as $\{L_1, L_2, \ldots, L_n, L_{n+1}, \ldots, L_N\}$ and $\{l_1, l_2, \ldots, l_n, l_{n+1}, \ldots, l_N\}$. Constructing an MPI vector requires three major inputs: counts, blocklength and strides. We treat each array element as an individual block, so the blocklength is set to always be 1. There will be l_n blocks of $A_{i_1, i_2, \ldots, i_n}$ on dimension n to constitute the higher dimensional array $A_{i_1, i_2, \ldots, i_{n+1}}$. The interval between each n-d array is the axis length of the original array L_n, which feeds to the stride parameter. In this way, a subarray of N dimensions is constructed recursively.

We leverage `MPI_Type_hvector`, a heterogeneous version of `MPI_Type_vector`, where the stride is interpreted in bytes. This enables the insertion of subarrays belonging to the same dimension into the gaps within each other.

To support arbitrary storage orders, we shuffle the nesting order to align with the given order. Additionally, an offset is calculated based on the `array_of_starts` argument. We then use `MPI_Type_hindexed` to append this offset, resulting in the final derived datatype. Figure 1 shows an example of creating 2 different storage orders from the same shape of subarray.

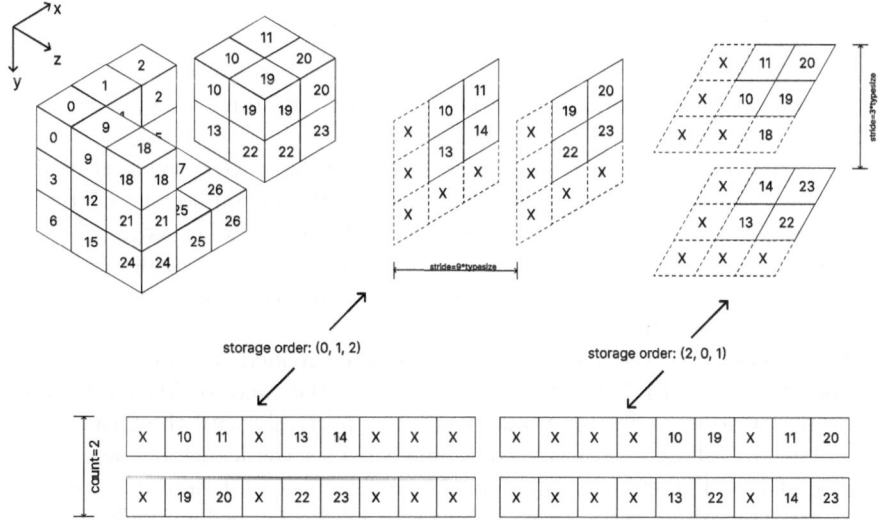

Fig. 1. Illustration of creating 3D subarrays for orders $(0, 1, 2)$ and $(2, 0, 1)$. Elements 10, 11, 13, 14, 19, 20, 22, 23 are extracted from a $3 \times 3 \times 3$ array. To build a subarray ordered $(0, 1, 2)$ using existing 2D arrays ordered $(0, 1)$, the 2D plane has a stride of 9, derived from the product of the lengths of axes 0 and 1. In the $(2, 0, 1)$ order, the final axis, 1, results in a stride equal to the length of the previous axis, (0), which is 3. Both ordered arrays contain 2 lower-level 2D arrays, corresponding to the length of the final axis of the subarray being 2. X represents the element that is vacant in corresponding positions.

4   Experimental Platform

Experiments were run on resources owned by the Digital Research Alliance of Canada. For our experiments we used Narval, a system with an Infiniband Mellanox HDR network, 2 AMD Rome 7532 CPUs, each with 32 cores, running Rocky Linux 8.9 and Open MPI 4.1.5. AMD Rome 7532 has cores with 32 KB L1 data cache, 512 KB L2 cache and a 256 MB shared L3 cache. All of the following experiments were repeated 10 times to achieve an average.

5   Balancing Communication and Computation Efficiency

Our proposed method uses a more complicated communication exchange in order to accelerate computational efficiency when the data has been received. To better understand what the benefits of different memory layouts for 3D FFT solves are, as well as the differences in communication performance, we analyze them here before we conduct performance evaluation on our proposed method in Sect. 6.

5.1   Measuring the Penalty of Strided FFT

We use slab composition to illustrate the effect of strided memory access in distributed 3D FFT computation. The initial array is stored in xyz row-major order with a global size of $\{L_x, L_y, L_z\}$.

First, the global array is divided into slabs along the z-axis, and a series of 2D FFTs are performed on the xy plane. Subsequently, to compute the FFT along the last axis (z), the global array is redistributed along another axis, either x or y. In this process, if the storage order remains unchanged, the stride of the FFT along the z-axis becomes $L_x \cdot L_y$, compared to 1 in a contiguous array where z is the major storage rank.

To evaluate the performance difference between strided and contiguous memory operations with FFT, we tested 1D FFT along the z axis on 3D arrays stored in row-major order and column-major order respectively with the former yielding a strided FFT and the latter contiguous. We set the length of the z axis to be fixed at 128. Therefore, a single contiguous complex FFT on the z axis spans 2KB over the address space (each `FFTW_COMPLEX` comprises two doubles), while the strided version has a spanning of $2 \times L_x \times L_y$ KB which increases as the xy plane size grows.

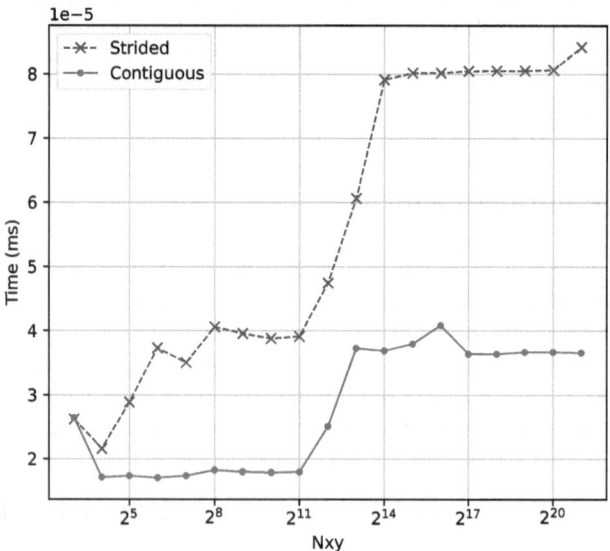

Fig. 2. Average Single FFT Time in the z Direction: Strided vs. Contiguous Access, $L_z = 128$

This test was done on a single core on Narval. The total computation time was recorded, and an average of a single FFT time on the z axis was calculated for comparison. We use `fftw_plan_many_dft` from FFTW library [9] for efficient

1D FFT. FFTW offers several planning flags: FFTW_ESTIMATE, FFTW_MEASURE, FFTW_PATIENT and FFTW_EXHAUSTIVE. FFTW_ESTIMATE chooses the computation strategy without running experiments, which means that it has the smallest plan creation time of the methods but incurs inferior computation performance. The rest of the planning flags are instead based on actual testing, distinguished by the comprehensiveness of the trial. We choose FFTW_MEASURE for its balanced efficiency in both plan creation and computation time.

In the test case, the execution time for the strided FFT in the z direction experiences two significant increases when N_{xy} is in the ranges of $(2^4, 2^8)$ and $(2^{11}, 2^{14})$. Additionally, the runtime for the contiguous FFT also rose when N_{xy} was between 2^{11} and 2^{13}. These increases can be attributed to two main factors:

1. When the size of the xy plane is relatively small, multiple arrays of 1D FFT data can fit into the cache. However, as N_{xy} increases, a smaller proportion of the total data can be loaded into the cache at once, thus reducing efficiency.
2. When the size of the xy plane is relatively large, a complete 1D strided FFT array can no longer fit in the cache.

In general, the strided FFT takes approximately twice as long as the contiguous FFT when N_{xy} exceeds 2^8. This is because strided data spans a wider range of addresses than contiguous data, leading to decreased cache efficiency. Therefore, avoiding unnecessary strided access to the data is essential in the computation stage.

5.2   Finding the Optimal Sending/Receiving DDT Pair

In a 3D array, there are a total of $3! = 6$ possible storage orderings. If we need to reorder the least major storage ranking (axis 2) to the major storage ranking (axis 0), we can configure the MPI storage order on the sending side as $(1, 2, 0)$ with the receiving side being ordered as $(2, 0, 1)$. This arrangement ensures that on the sending side, the elements on axis 2 (corresponding to the z axis) are packed in the middle position. Conversely, on the receiving side, the data, which are strided as the middle position, are unpacked by axis 0 (the x axis). Therefore, a $xyz - yzx$ local transpose is performed within the context of the alltoall communication. One can visualize these ordering differences like a reorganized cube during the process. While a Rubik's Cube is not a perfect analogy it provides a good visualization analogue for basic understanding; we are re-arranging the mini-cubes inside the larger problem to place all of the data needed for the next computation stage in contiguous memory. As we need to move data for communication anyways, adding in some additional communication complexity to make the computation phase faster is a viable option. As FFTW does work to arrive at the best approach to calculate the FFT, we move data with the best approach for calculating the FFT in the next phase. We will evaluate the effectiveness of this approach on performance in Sect. 6.

In a distributed 3D FFT scenario, where we aim to transform the last axis z to fit the major storage order, there are a total of 12 possible combinations of sending/receiving order pairs as listed on Table 1a.

Table 1. Global Redistribution time using unconventional storage order pairs and comparison against MPI default subarray under a $2048 \times 2048 \times 2048$ complex 3D array on Narval.

Id	Send/Recv Order	Cores	Time(s)
0	$(0, 1, \mathbf{2}) \rightarrow (1, 2, \mathbf{0})$	32	7.47
1	$(0, 1, \mathbf{2}) \rightarrow (2, 1, \mathbf{0})$	32	11.72
2	$(0, \mathbf{2}, 1) \rightarrow (1, \mathbf{0}, 2)$	32	**4.40**
3	$(0, \mathbf{2}, 1) \rightarrow (2, \mathbf{0}, 1)$	32	11.67
4	$(1, 0, \mathbf{2}) \rightarrow (1, 2, \mathbf{0})$	32	11.60
5	$(1, 0, \mathbf{2}) \rightarrow (2, 1, \mathbf{0})$	32	22.23
6	$(1, \mathbf{2}, 0) \rightarrow (1, \mathbf{0}, 2)$	32	11.57
7	$(1, \mathbf{2}, 0) \rightarrow (2, \mathbf{0}, 1)$	32	21.39
8	$(\mathbf{2}, 1, 0) \rightarrow (\mathbf{0}, 1, 2)$	32	10.48
9	$(\mathbf{2}, 1, 0) \rightarrow (\mathbf{0}, 2, 1)$	32	10.50
10	$(\mathbf{2}, 0, 1) \rightarrow (\mathbf{0}, 1, 2)$	32	9.62
11	$(\mathbf{2}, 0, 1) \rightarrow (\mathbf{0}, 2, 1)$	32	9.66

(a) Communication time using different sending/receiving storage orders

Cores	Size/Core	MPI default subarray(s)	Ours(s)	Increase
32	128GB	3.79	4.40	16.09%
64	64GB	1.76	1.93	9.66%
128	32GB	0.87	1.08	24.14%
256	16GB	0.65	0.68	4.62%
512	8GB	0.39	0.52	33.33%

(b) Communication performance comparison between MPI default subarray (MPI_ORDER_C) and our sending/receiving order pair $(0, 2, 1) \rightarrow (1, 0, 2)$ with different number of cores involved.

In this method, performance degradation is expected to occur compared to using the same storage order on both the sending and receiving sides. Although the type maps on both sides match, and the alltoall transpose is effective, the datatype engine expends extra effort in packing and shifting elements to their designated positions after unpacking. To assess this, we tested a $2048 \times 2048 \times 2048$ complex 3D array, totalling 4096 GB in size, for redistribution operation from x axis to z axis with a total of 32 cores.

Table 1a displays the communication overhead of all 12 possible combinations, showing a notable performance variation ranging from 4.40 to 22.23 s. Among these, the unconventional orders $(0, 2, 1) \rightarrow (1, 0, 2)$ incur minimal overhead during the redistribution phase and are therefore selected for comparison with `MPI_Type_create_subarray` using `MPI_ORDER_C`. Table 1b illustrates the increased communication time of using different storage orders on the sending/receiving side, varying from 4.62% to 33.33%.

Compared to the penalties associated with strided FFT, utilizing a shuffled storage order on both the sending and receiving sides is advantageous when the appropriate pair is chosen. This is because, under the same size/core configuration, the time saved by using a contiguous FFT significantly outweighs the time increase due to the shuffled storage order. In the Sect. 6, we will compare the overall performance of our method with Dalcin's method in a complex distributed 3D FFT computation.

6   Performance Evaluation

To evaluate the performance of our method, we will use identical datatypes for collective communication and perform strong scaling and weak scaling tests with slab decomposition. For the slab decomposition, the 3D array is stored in a row-major order where the z axis has the fastest varying index. Specifically, the global data is first partitioned along the z axis for 2D FFTs on xy planes and then partitioned along the x axis for 1D FFTs on the z axis.

For communication, we used `MPI_Alltoallw` for the data redistribution. For computation, we continue to use `fftw_plan_many_dft` from Sect. 5 to plan for multiple 2D and 1D FFTs.

6.1   Strong Scaling

For the strong scaling test, we use a $2048 \times 2048 \times 2048$ cubic array arranged over varying core counts ranging from 32 to 1024 cores. Because of the limited memory of 256GB of a single node of Narval, we do not use full cores on the node, leaving some cores idle in order to have more memory for the working cores.

Figure 3a shows the overall 3D FFT processing time. In this figure, the performance of our method(using different datatypes in collective communication) is represented by a solid red line with the label "Asymmetrical" while that of using MPI default subarrays use a dotted blue line with label "Identical" for its use of same storage order. In Fig. 3b, two types of speedup are calculated: the first is computational speedup, which only compares the running time of the FFTW library, and the second is total speedup, which compares the overall execution time of the two methods. These speedups are represented by a solid purple line and a dotted green line, respectively.

In terms of computational speed up, our method has a computation speed up from 1.51X to, notably 3.12X at a core count of 1024. Typically communication does not scale well as the core number increases, and it becomes the major overhead when the core count is relatively large. This was considered a challenge for our method because we sacrificed part of the communication performance for the benefit of better data arrangement. The results show that our method managed to maintain its advantage with large core counts, resulting in an overall speedup between 1.17X and 1.44X, with 1.44X occurring at 64 cores. We note that the speedup advantage spikes significantly at 1024 cores, but overall speedup remains within expected range due to higher communication overheads.

Re-examining Fig. 2, we see that the single FFT time rises dramatically between FFTs of sizes 2^{11} and 2^{13}. It is reasonable that the spike of computation spike occurs when problem size reaches the better performance tier in certain core counts.

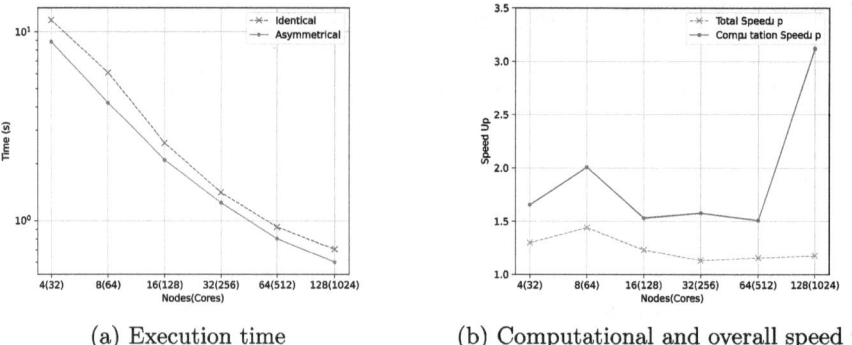

(a) Execution time   (b) Computational and overall speed up

Fig. 3. Strong scaling test of $2048 \times 2048 \times 2048$ complex FFT on Narval.

6.2   Weak Scaling

For weak scaling tests, we double the length of each axis in turn for each test, resulting in global data shapes ranging from 512^3 to 2048^3. Core count is doubled along with data size. We run 2 sets of weak scaling tests, one with core numbers from 16 to 1024 and the other from 32 to 2048. The two sets of tests reflect weak scaling of different unit data sizes per core.

In both sets of experiments, our method has a shorter running time. However, the speed up trend is different. In the first set of weak scaling tests where each core having a smaller unit size of data, the speed up decreases gradually from its peak of 1.19X to 1.04X. In the second set of tests, the computational speed up increases significantly when cores are greater than 512, spiking at 9.36X when the core number is 2048 in accordance with a 2.2X overall speed up at this point.

There are various factors leading to the fluctuation of computational and overall speed up both in the strong scaling test and weak scaling test. First is the non-linear scalability of collective communication, which becomes less efficient as the data communication becomes fragmented when each core holds a small amount of data. Second, the speed-up of contiguous array is dependent on the utilization conditions of different layers of cache. The data shape also has an influence on the computation speed, which is why we see variations in performance as the problem expands with the resources allocated. Once again we see greater speedups at larger core counts. This is an artifact with weak scaling of data shape, something that the strong scaling tests did not encounter. While we could not run problems greater than 2048 cores due to resource limitations we expect that performance may decline from its peaks due to problem size shape with larger problems (Fig. 4).

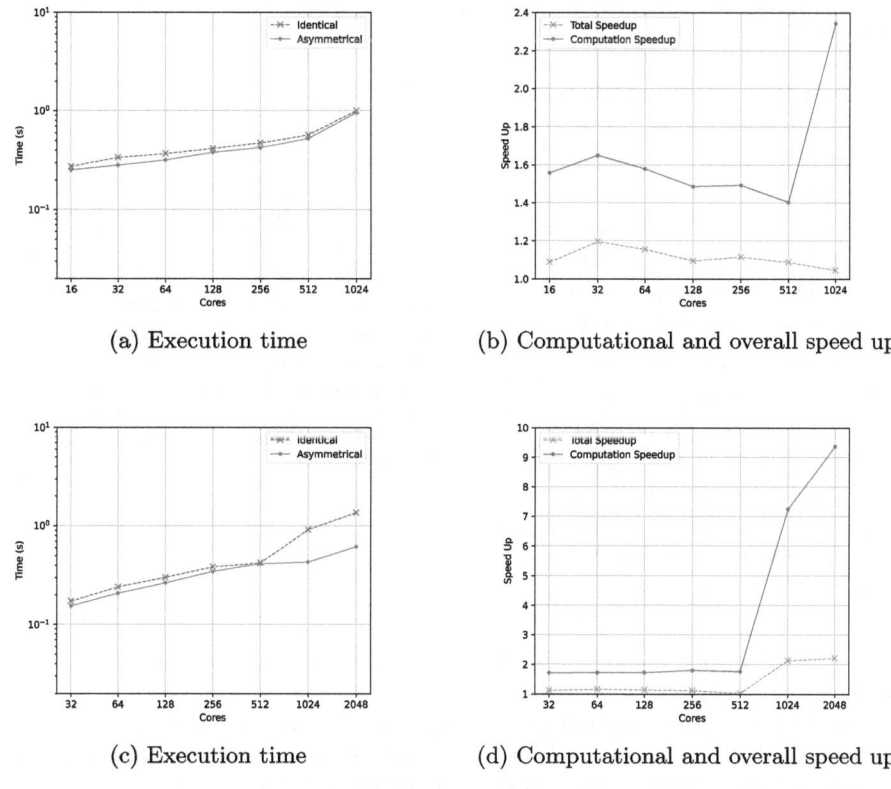

(a) Execution time

(b) Computational and overall speed up

(c) Execution time

(d) Computational and overall speed up

Fig. 4. Weak Scaling test results on Narval, (a) and (b): Execution time and speed up for cores ranging from 16 to 1024. (c) and (d): Execution time and speed up for cores ranging from 32 to 2048

6.3   Communication Performance on Beluga

The experiments conducted on Narval demonstrated the benefits of using asymmetrical datatypes for communication. In order to demonstrate the generality of our approach, we will test if ordering pairs have the same best performing storage order. To determine if the ordering is stable for collective communication across different systems we conduct tests on a different platform, Beluga, another computer operated by the Alliance.

Beluga is equipped with 2 Xeon Gold 6148 CPUs on each node, using a Mellanox InfiniBand EDR network. It operates with the same software stack as Narval (Table 2).

For our experiments we find the optimal sending/receiving pair is prone to change with regard to the specific hardware and software configuration. On Beluga, the best transform option is to use storage order $(2, 0, 1)$ on the sending side and $(0, 2, 1)$ on the receiving side. Therefore, it is advised that trial experi-

Table 2. Global Redistribution time using unconventional storage order pairs and comparison against MPI default subarray under a $2000 \times 2000 \times 2000$ complex 3D array on Beluga.

Id	Send/Recv Order	Cores	Time(s)
0	$(0,1,2) \rightarrow (1,2,0)$	40	8.73
1	$(0,1,2) \rightarrow (2,1,0)$	40	11.86
2	$(0,2,1) \rightarrow (1,0,2)$	40	4.60
3	$(0,2,1) \rightarrow (2,0,1)$	40	6.45
4	$(1,0,2) \rightarrow (1,2,0)$	40	10.62
5	$(1,0,2) \rightarrow (2,1,0)$	40	10.41
6	$(1,2,0) \rightarrow (1,0,2)$	40	9.82
7	$(1,2,0) \rightarrow (2,0,1)$	40	9.75
8	$(2,1,0) \rightarrow (0,1,2)$	40	5.35
9	$(2,1,0) \rightarrow (0,2,1)$	40	5.39
10	$(2,0,1) \rightarrow (0,1,2)$	40	4.22
11	$(2,0,1) \rightarrow (0,2,1)$	40	**4.18**

(a) Communication time using different sending/receiving storage orders

Cores	Size/Core	MPI default subarray(s)	Ours	Increase
40	128GB	3.72	4.18	12.38%
80	64GB	1.89	2.05	8.42%
160	32GB	1.17	1.49	27.9%
320	16GB	0.79	0.88	11.54%
640	8GB	0.78	0.81	2.93%

(b) Communication time comparison of MPI default subarray (MPI_ORDER_C) and the best candidate among unconventional send/receive pairs.

ments be performed to probe the best strategy before using asymmetrical communication datatypes on a system.

On Beluga, using asymmetrical datatypes has a maximum performance increase of 27.9% over the default MPI subarray with 160 cores communicating over a $2000 \times 2000 \times 2000$ array, compared to 33.3% on Narval.

7 Related Work

Previous work has studied the performance of MPI derived datatypes [4,19], yet the investigation is limited to basic data layouts where nested datatype with order is not considered. The application of DDT on GPUs are developed by Jenkins et al. [13] and Suresh et al. [17] with the former implementing data packing kernel for MPI datatypes in GPU and the latter improving the GPU datatype processing with the assistance of HCA (Host Channel Adapter).

Various distributed FFT libraries have been developed with different data movement strategies. P3DFFT [15] employs pencil decomposition to provide higher scalability where its data packing is explicit. AccFFT [10] and heFFT [3] are developed for heterogeneous architecture, both of them perform packing and communication at the same time.

The communication time cost of parallel FFT is extensively studied. Theoretical and empirical modeling for time consumption are studied by Czechowski et al. [7] and Ayala et al. [2]. Other techniques for optimizing communication overhead include adjusting job placement concerning a given physical network topology [1].

Past work has looked at user derived datatypes in MPI [4] and improving their performance [11] even with GPUs [13]. Recent optimizations of collectives occurred in work by Sewell et al. [16].

8   Conclusions

In our study, we developed a constructor subarray datatype, supporting arbitrary storage order. By using this function, we are able to incorporate the local reordering operation in a global alltoall communication, avoiding strided access for data in parallel 3D FFT computation. We have demonstrated the benefits of using alternative storage order pairs on the sending/receiving side to achieve the same transposition effect with improved performance. The results on Narval show our method is preferable compared to using identical datatypes in communication as the time gained by consecutive FFT outweigh the time loss of asymmetry datatype processing, having a total speedup of 1.17x to 1.44x in the strong scaling test by speeding up the computation phase by up to 3.12x. Further tests show that different ordering pairs are beneficial on different systems, finding that having the flexibility to choose different ordering pairs is important to overall FFT performance.

Acknowledgments. We acknowledge the support of the Natural Sciences and Engineering Research Council of Canada (NSERC), [funding reference number ALLRP 578539-2022] and the Digital Research Alliance of Canada. This research was enabled in part by support provided by the Digital Research Alliance of Canada.

References

1. Aseeri, S.A., Gopal Chatterjee, A., Verma, M.K., Keyes, D.E.: A scheduling policy to save 10% of communication time in parallel fast Fourier transform. Concurrency Comput. Pract. Experience **35**(15), e6508 (2023). https://doi.org/10.1002/cpe.6508. https://onlinelibrary.wiley.com/doi/abs/10.1002/cpe.6508
2. Ayala, A., Tomov, S., Stoyanov, M., Haidar, A., Dongarra, J.: Accelerating multi - process communication for parallel 3-D FFT. In: 2021 Workshop on Exascale MPI (ExaMPI), pp. 46–53 (2021). https://doi.org/10.1109/ExaMPI54564.2021.00011
3. Ayala, A., Tomov, S., Haidar, A., Dongarra, J.: *heFFTe*: highly efficient FFT for exascale. In: Krzhizhanovskaya, V.V., et al. (eds.) ICCS 2020. LNCS, vol. 12137, pp. 262–275. Springer, Cham (2020). https://doi.org/10.1007/978-3-030-50371-0_19
4. Carpen-Amarie, A., Hunold, S., Träff, J.L.: On the expected and observed communication performance with MPI derived datatypes. In: Proceedings of the 23rd European MPI Users' Group Meeting, EuroMPI 2016, pp. 108–120. Association for Computing Machinery, New York, NY, USA (2016). https://doi.org/10.1145/2966884.2966905
5. Chatterjee, A.G., Verma, M.K., Kumar, A., Samtaney, R., Hadri, B., Khurram, R.: Scaling of a fast Fourier transform and a pseudo-spectral fluid solver up to 196608 cores. J. Parallel Distrib. Comput. **113**, 77–91 (2018). https://doi.org/10.1016/j.jpdc.2017.10.014. https://www.sciencedirect.com/science/article/pii/S0743731517302903

6. Cooley, J.W., Tukey, J.W.: An algorithm for the machine calculation of complex Fourier series. Math. Comput. **19**, 297–301 (1965). http://cr.yp.to/bib/entries.html#1965/cooley

7. Czechowski, K., Battaglino, C., McClanahan, C., Iyer, K., Yeung, P.K., Vuduc, R.: On the communication complexity of 3D FFTs and its implications for exascale. In: Proceedings of the 26th ACM International Conference on Supercomputing, ICS 2012, pp. 205–214. Association for Computing Machinery, New York, NY, USA (2012). https://doi.org/10.1145/2304576.2304604

8. Dalcin, L., Mortensen, M., Keyes, D.E.: Fast parallel multidimensional FFT using advanced MPI. J. Parallel Distributed Comput. **128**, 137–150 (2019). https://doi.org/10.1016/j.jpdc.2019.02.006. https://www.sciencedirect.com/science/article/pii/S074373151830306X

9. Frigo, M., Johnson, S.G.: The design and implementation of FFTW3. Proc. IEEE **93**(2), 216–231 (2005). Special issue on "Program Generation, Optimization, and Platform Adaptation"

10. Gholami, A., Hill, J., Malhotra, D., Biros, G.: AccFFT: a library for distributed-memory FFT on CPU and GPU architectures (2016)

11. Gropp, W., Lusk, E., Swider, D.: Improving the performance of MPI derived datatypes. In: Proceedings of the Third MPI Developer's and User's Conference, pp. 25–30. Citeseer (1999)

12. Hoefler, T., Gottlieb, S.: Parallel zero-copy algorithms for fast Fourier transform and conjugate gradient using MPI datatypes. In: Keller, R., Gabriel, E., Resch, M., Dongarra, J. (eds.) EuroMPI 2010. LNCS, vol. 6305, pp. 132–141. Springer, Heidelberg (2010). https://doi.org/10.1007/978-3-642-15646-5_14

13. Jenkins, J., Dinan, J., Balaji, P., Peterka, T., Samatova, N.F., Thakur, R.: Processing MPI derived datatypes on noncontiguous GPU-resident data. IEEE Trans. Parallel Distrib. Syst. **25**(10), 2627–2637 (2013). https://doi.org/10.1109/TPDS.2013.234

14. Jung, J., Kobayashi, C., Imamura, T., Sugita, Y.: Parallel implementation of 3D FFT with volumetric decomposition schemes for efficient molecular dynamics simulations. Comput. Phys. Commun. **200**, 57–65 (2016). https://doi.org/10.1016/j.cpc.2015.10.024. https://www.sciencedirect.com/science/article/pii/S0010465515004063

15. Pekurovsky, D.: P3DFFT: a framework for parallel computations of Fourier transforms in three dimensions. SIAM J. Sci. Comput. **34**(4), C192–C209 (2012). https://doi.org/10.1137/11082748X

16. Sewell, A., Fan, K., Shovon, A.R., Dyken, L., Kumar, S., Petruzza, S.: Bruck algorithm performance analysis for multi-GPU all-to-all communication. In: Proceedings of the International Conference on High Performance Computing in Asia-Pacific Region, pp. 127–133 (2024)

17. Suresh, K.K., et al.: Network assisted non-contiguous transfers for GPU-aware MPI libraries. In: 2022 IEEE Symposium on High-Performance Interconnects (HOTI), pp. 13–20 (2022). https://doi.org/10.1109/HOTI55740.2022.00018

18. Turnes, C.K., Romberg, J.: Spiral FFT: an efficient method for 3-D FFTs on spiral MRI contours. In: 2010 IEEE International Conference on Image Processing, pp. 617–620 (2010). https://doi.org/10.1109/ICIP.2010.5653254

19. Xiong, Q., Bangalore, P.V., Skjellum, A., Herbordt, M.: MPI derived datatypes: performance and portability issues. In: Proceedings of the 25th European MPI Users' Group Meeting, EuroMPI 2018. Association for Computing Machinery, New York, NY, USA (2018). https://doi.org/10.1145/3236367.3236378

To Share or Not to Share: A Case for MPI in Shared-Memory

Julien Adam[1]([✉]), Jean-Baptiste Besnard[1], Adrien Roussel[2,3], Julien Jaeger[2,3], Patrick Carribault[2,3], and Marc Pérache[2,3]

[1] ParaTools SAS, Bruyères-le-Châtel, France
adamj@paratools.com
[2] CEA, DAM, DIF, 91297 Arpajon, France
[3] Université Paris-Saclay, CEA, Laboratoire en Informatique Haute Performance pour le Calcul et la simulation, 91680 Bruyères-le-Châtel, France

Abstract. The evolution of parallel computing architectures presents new challenges for developing efficient parallelized codes. The emergence of heterogeneous systems has given rise to multiple programming models, each requiring careful adaptation to maximize performance. In this context, we propose reevaluating memory layout designs for computational tasks within larger nodes by comparing various architectures. To gain insight into the performance discrepancies between shared memory and shared-address space settings, we systematically measure the bandwidth between cores and sockets using different methodologies. Our findings reveal significant differences in performance, suggesting that MPI running inside UNIX processes may not fully utilize its intranode bandwidth potential. In light of our work in the MPC thread-based MPI runtime, which can leverage shared memory to achieve higher performance due to its optimized layout, we advocate for enabling the use of shared memory within the MPI standard.

Keywords: MPI · NUMA · Memory · Thread · Programming Models

1 Introduction

The parallel programming landscape has undergone significant changes in recent decades, posing challenges for developers working on long-standing applications. Initially relying solely on Message Passing Interface (MPI) for distributed memory parallelism, the evolution of hardware and increasing node complexity has necessitated the adoption of hybrid MPI+X models such as OpenMP for shared memory parallelism since the early 2000s. This trend is likely to persist through the development of more powerful nodes while memory per core decreases.

Moreover, the emergence of converged or topologically-sensitive hardware, characterized by Non-Uniform Memory Access (NUMA), has added another layer of complexity to parallel programming. Writing efficient codes in such environments is crucial for minimizing data movement across the memory hierarchy. This requirement often necessitates the use of multiple programming models, including distributed and shared memory paradigms, as well as a thorough understanding of the hardware.

While these concepts are well-documented in literature, navigating this complex landscape with existing code while preserving performance remains an open research question. In this paper, we pose the question of the role of MPI in managing data locality. It is clear that, in its default form, MPI is NUMA-aware, as it creates separate processes with clear bindings. However, as we will further elaborate in the rest of this paper, communication between Unix processes is suboptimal in shared-memory configurations. After measuring this difference on recent hardware, we argue that having shared-memory communication primitives in MPI could be beneficial given the increasing size of nodes and their heterogeneity—requiring careful computing spatialization.

2   Background and Motivation

In this paper, we focus specifically on shared memory programming with increasingly large nodes that require hybridization. We first recall how programming interfaces are evolving to accommodate multiple models in a single application. Then, we discuss the contribution of our research; questioning the position of MPI in this model nesting and suggesting it could also apply to shared-memory systems. Furthermore, we touch upon existing methods for moving data inside and between processes on a single node.

2.1   On the Evolution of Programming Interfaces

When examining legacy applications with respect to parallel computing using shared memory, it has become increasingly specialized over time to reveal hierarchical parallelism. With GPUs emerging as the preferred choice for energy-efficient computing, an additional layer has been introduced to the hardware stack. As a result, vendor-specific interfaces are commonly employed due to their extensive support and efficiency compared to portable alternatives such as OpenMP Targets. This inclination towards higher-level, vendor-supported interfaces supports the development of abstraction layers like Kokkos in C++ [28], aiming to conceal the underlying differences to ease adoption and efficient parallelization.

MPI has long been the go-to choice for high-performance computing applications due to its widespread adoption. However, in the realm of machine learning, vendors have adopted smaller subsets of MPI into their vendor-specific libraries such as NCCL, RCCL, and oneCCL [32]. This shift can be attributed to several reasons. Firstly, the complexity of MPI and its lack of native support for GPUs–essential components in ML–could be a significant factor. The expectations of end-users for drop-in implementations may have further motivated vendors to develop customized solutions better suited to their hardware and topologies [5].

Abstracting these optimizations into standard interfaces is challenging in the face of industry competition.

Back to the context of HPC, MPI remains the de facto standard for distributing computations. Its stability and rigorous standardization make MPI reliable for long-running production applications historically used in high-performance computing landscapes. However, we argue that MPI requires significant evolutions to maintain its position as the preferred embedding model for modern HPC workloads. We refer to MPI as the *embedding model* because when a parallel program is initiated, it begins with UNIX processes operating under the batch manager, which are subsequently assigned ranks to establish a logical mapping of processes (a specific rank within `MPI_COMM_WORLD`). MPI plays a pivotal role in defining how jobs are structured and executed, while applications are constructed around its abstraction. Moreover, programs can further subdivide each logical unit using in-memory parallel programming models like OpenMP. In cases where necessary, they can even incorporate GPU code through the utilization of optimized BLAS libraries or by transferring part of the code to GPUs using frameworks such as CUDA, ROCm, or oneAPI.

2.2   Means of Moving and Sharing Memory in Linux

The long history of MPI has been instrumental in driving the development and exploration of not just data movement over high-performance networks, but also within nodes, i.e., between Unix processes. As such, at the node level, the MPI runtime provides a means to move small messages using shared memory segments (SHM) [4]. These segments are structured as message queues between MPI processes, with the same pages projected into the address space of multiple processes. When an MPI process sends or receives a message, it first copies the data into the shared-memory segment before copying from the segment and placing it in the final buffer. This necessarily leads to two separate copies of the same data: one in the segment, another from the segment. It should be noted that MPI's main messaging interface, designed for distributed memory, always involves copying message data from one buffer to another, leading to duplication of information.

Despite shared memory being the preferred approach for small messages due to its efficiency, larger messages require a different method. The projected memory region has a fixed size, thus fragmentation is necessary if SHM is used, leading to unnecessary copies and extra overhead. Alternative approaches include using DMA-capable network cards to perform local DMA for copy operations. If these methods are not feasible, the Linux kernel can be used as a trusted third-party to carry out memory copies across process address spaces. These interfaces, such as Cross-Memory Attach (CMA) [31], which is standard in Linux and performs cross-address space copies, take an IOVEC and a process ID to perform the copy. Similar interfaces, including KNEM [10], LiMIC [16], or more recently XPMEM [30], with improved performance or support for DMA engines such as I/O AT were also developed as kernel modules due to their need to securely bridge process address spaces.

2.3 Contribution

In the face of escalating demands for parallel programming models and divergent development approaches, it is imperative to recognize the necessity of advanced abstraction layers to ensure feasible and manageable program development. By abstracting away complexity, we can maintain productive development processes despite intricate underlying architectures. However, existing methods employing nested abstractions present significant challenges in both programming and performance optimization.

To substantiate this argument, we conduct a series of experiments using openly available codes[1] to evaluate the performance disparities between shared-memory and shared-address spaces on contemporary hardware platforms such as the Nvidia Grace Superchip and Intel Sapphire Rapids. Following earlier research by Hori et al. [13], we also conclude that for communication-intensive and/or memory-bound applications, MPI executed within UNIX processes is unable to fully tap into its potential on these devices – requiring a single process per node to take advantage of full bandwidth capabilities.

Our intention is not to propose a definitive solution to this predicament. Instead, we draw attention to various remedies that have been proposed in the literature (including our past work) and discuss potential enhancements to MPI, such as enhanced awareness of shared-memory execution, which could better exploit its capabilities.

3 Performance Measurement Approach

In this section, we outline our approach for evaluating memory transfer performance, focusing on empirical methods. Our tests aim to explore the bandwidth between different locations. Measuring latency typically involves exchanging small messages and calculating the round-trip time. Alternatively, bandwidth can be estimated by determining the duration required for a message of known size to transfer. However, in practice, gauging bandwidth proves simpler than assessing latency due to its role as a bandwidth penalty during transfer initiation. To bypass these costs, we opt for large data transfers (exceeding 1 MB) in our experiments. The bandwidth results are then averaged from N transfer trials to eliminate the impact of initialization. Based on the proposed practical data transfer model, our study aims to investigate the effectiveness of various data transfer methods across several representative architectures, such as NVIDIA Grace Superchips and Intel Sapphire Rapids. This allows us to evaluate the performance of inter-core connectivity and the quality of cross-chip interconnects. To achieve this goal, we ask the question: how can a program optimally utilize this interconnect and bandwidth using standard system interfaces, including MPI? To answer this question, we conducted measurements to determine both sequential and parallel core-to-core bandwidth within and between sockets.

---

[1] https://github.com/besnardjb/memmapper.

The measurements we conducted enable us to assess the cost difference between a shared-memory approach (using memcpy) and a shared-address space method utilizing the Cross-Memory Attach interface on our selected architectures. Although interfaces such as XPMEM [13, 30] may offer better performance, they were not available in our test environment. However, these interfaces still require a kernel mitigation to project the remote address space into the local one, which comes with its own cost and necessitates caching by MPI for optimal efficiency. Once implemented, this can be viewed as an on-demand shared memory segment, ensuring high performance. During this process, we also examine the data-movement performance of MPI, which is the de facto standard for moving data between processes in HPC. Hybrid approaches such as MPI+OpenMP still leverage the same fundamental data transfer technologies relying on methods like memcpies for exchanging information and the reason we chose to focus on pure MPI.

The idea behind these measures is to contextualize how well data can be moved across various architectures. Of course, there are other performance parameters, such as latency and operations per cycle. We do not purport to cover all aspects of the performance spectrum. In fact, some applications may not be sensitive to bandwidth and might instead be more computing-bound. However, in the case of MPI, which is focused on moving data around, our goal is to identify a measurable parameter (in this case, bandwidth), project it onto multiple architectures, outline overall performance improvements, and demonstrate the ability of interfaces to harvest maximum performance.

3.1 Sequential Shared-Memory Core-to-Core Bandwidth

When considering two cores exchanging data in point-to-point communication, what is the achievable bandwidth? To measure this, we set up a system where data segments are mapped to specific cores with proper affinity. We then copy that data to a buffer local to another processing unit while repeating these steps for the entire system. This measures the sequential bandwidth (as only one transfer occurs at a time) between cores, which is a common and basic measurement in many computer systems used as a baseline to evaluate the performance of the memory subsystems. We have developed a simple `memmapper`[2] tool, which can carry out this procedure with configurable sizes.

Looking at Fig. 1, it is noticeable that NUMA effects have a significant impact on memory bandwidths between cores. As nodes become larger, the memory hierarchy also becomes more complex. For example, looking at the figure depicting 1 MB transfers on the Grace Superchip (top left), one can see how the performance differs without considering cache effects when the data size increases to 100 MB (bottom left). As expected, this analysis reveals that spatializing processing correctly can significantly enhance data transfer rates and reduce bottlenecks when performing concurrent transfers between cores. However, the question that arises from these measurements is whether this behavior remains

---

[2] https://github.com/besnardjb/memmapper.

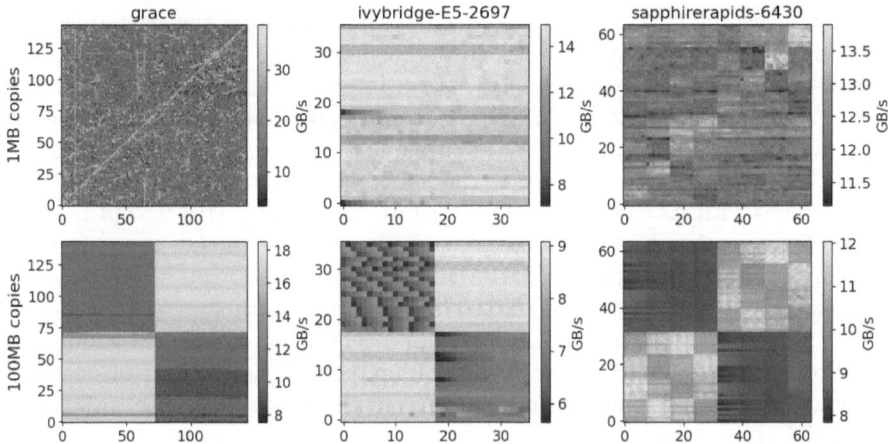

Fig. 1. Outline of NUMA effects on various architectures and transfer sizes. Coordinates (x, y) denotes data transfers from core x to core y. Color represents averaged bandwidth over 1000 transfers.

consistent when conducting several parallel transfers, or if there are any bottlenecks. To this purpose, in the next section, we will compare both CMA and memcpy when performing parallel data-transfers, which are more representative of HPC payloads.

3.2 Parallel Shared-Memory Core-to-Core Bandwidth

We repeated these measurements by creating data-transfer pairs between cores located in the same socket and across different sockets. To achieve this, we prepared buffers and synchronously initiated the transfers. The measured bandwidth is the average of the bandwidths over the entire duration of each transfer, not an average of individual bandwidths. This approach accounts for temporal scattering of data transfers, as it is virtually impossible to ensure that all transfers start simultaneously and complete at the same time.

In Fig. 2, we present results for N concurrent data transfers within a given socket and between sockets of a particular architecture for both 1MB and 200 MB message sizes. These measurements were obtained using memory reuse, which involves averaging the bandwidth of 100 transfers of the same buffer after it has been bound to local affinity with a memset operation. Consequently, these measurements are susceptible to cache effects since the same data is copied multiple times. For instance, in Fig. 2 bottom left, when transferring between sockets, the total bandwidth reaches up to 1300 MB/s on Grace Superchip, which surpasses the theoretical peak of NVLink interconnect (900 GB/s) due to caching effects. However, this effect diminishes at larger sizes because cache effects decrease.

To clarify, until now, we have discussed how shared memory bandwidth has evolved within a single node in the context of a single address space. However, it

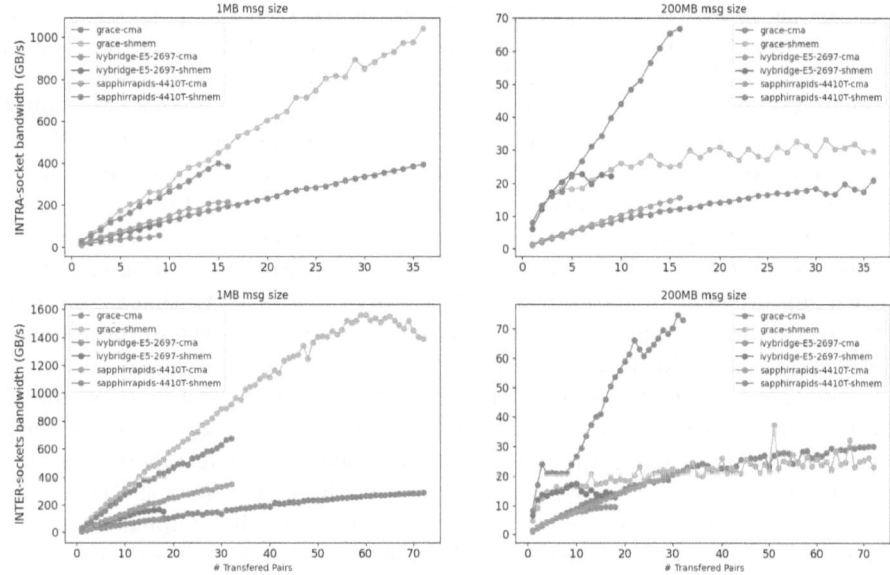

Fig. 2. Total bandwidth for concurrent transfers both inside and between sockets on various architectures using either Cross-Memory Attach or regular `memcpy` (shmem). All measurements are averaged 100 times.

is essential to note that MPI is designed to run on distributed memory systems, which means multiple processes need to exchange data efficiently both within a node and between nodes. While high-speed interconnects can be used for communication between nodes, intranode communications require different methods. For smaller messages, most MPI implementations employ shared memory segments, where data is copied into the segment and subsequently transferred to the destination buffer. However, this approach may not be efficient for larger messages due to potential fragmentation. As a result, for larger messages MPI primarily uses Cross-Memory Attach or its more advanced implementation KNEM for interprocess communication across different address spaces.

Table 1. Performance ratio between Shared-Memory and CMA for the largest number of concurrent copies, considering configurations of Fig. 2.

Size	Nvidia GRACE		Intel SAPPHIRE	
	Intra	Inter	Intra	Inter
1 MB	2.64	4.81	1.77	1.94
200 MB	1.41	0.76	4.28	3.43

Looking at Fig. 2, a comparison between shared-memory and CMA bandwidth reveals that the performance difference increases with the number of involved cores. This leads to significant performance differences, as shown in Table 1. We observe that Intel Sapphire and Nvidia Grace Superchip exhibit different responses. Overall, shared-memory improves performance by a factor of 2.63 on average compared to CMA. However, with larger copies, the transfer performance of Grace is significantly decreased when compared to messages fitting in caches, making CMA faster than `memcpy` in such cases. This is a singular result that we consider linked to saturation on the NVLINK, leading to performance improvements due to the extra overhead of CMAs alleviating contention. This hypothesis is supported by the noisier response of the system (despite the 100 averages), as evident from Fig. 2 bottom right.

Note that this performance difference can be mitigated with more advanced shared-address space mechanisms, such as XPMEM. However, we did not have access to systems of the given architecture with this module installed. Nonetheless, despite the ability to bypass the kernel in the copies once the pages are projected, there is still a need to set up segments (and thus implement a rendezvous protocol and necessary caching). This necessarily creates overhead for teardown and setup. As such, even though the bandwidth penalty would be reduced on a projected segment, the projection cost would remain, particularly for applications that frequently change buffers over time.

4   Adapting MPI to Shared-Memory

Given the observed performance difference between CMA and a shared-memory copy, we must consider the implications for MPI. MPI is designed for distributed memory systems, which run on multiple nodes; however, its support for shared memory might be limited due to its design. In this section, we will discuss potential solutions to address this situation. We start by recalling current shared-memory support in MPI. Then, we discuss how the standard may progressively incorporate support for shared-memory. Lastly, we recall alternative methods for porting MPI in shared-memory including process virtualization.

4.1   Current and Past Support for MPI in Shared-Memory

Although MPI has made significant strides forward with the introduction of version 4.0, support for shared-memory has remained relatively stagnant since MPI 3.0. One notable exception to this trend is the addition of MPI 3.0 shared-memory windows, which have enabled a shared address space to be projected between MPI processes running on the same node. This window mechanism represents an important step towards harnessing the performance benefits of shared memory within the context of the MPI paradigm. By enabling in-memory communication and collaboration between processes, these shared-memory windows can lead to improved efficiency and reduced latency in parallel computing applications that utilize both message passing and shared memory [12].

Moving forward, several mitigation strategies were introduced. The most notable advancement was in MPI 4.0's Partitioned Communications [7,9], which allowed multiple contributors to one communication. As matching is done at the initialization of the partitioned communication, the matching step can be removed and buffers can directly be moved to the destination.

FinePoints [11] were also considered, allowing for shared memory ranks to be added to a given rank in MPI, thus enabling MPI partitioned to work with shared-memory in a thread-aware manner. However, the Allocating Receive and Freeing Send operations [21] were initially considered but ultimately rejected by the MPI forum due to issues with implementing derived datatypes on such in-place transfers. Eventually, the proposal for an endpoint feature (the ability to add shared-memory ranks to a given rank), also known as MPI Endpoints [20], remained unfinished due to lack of consensus from the broader MPI community.

Overall, the most commonly used MPI interfaces are still copy-oriented and do not take advantage of a shared-memory setup, impeding memory duplication between the source and destination buffer. Furthermore, ways of numbering ranks within a shared-address space are not part of the standard, preventing the exploration of alternative copy-avoiding messaging mechanisms that might benefit from the performance gains we have exposed in previous sections. Consequently, MPI is bound to be avoided at the node level and limited to inter-node exchanges unless it can expose dedicated interfaces to efficiently address node-level topology. As an embedding programming model, being able to "name" threads bound to various localities within a given process may allow for finer-grain usage of nested programming models while facilitating software differentiation (workflows [19], MPMD [27], service oriented [25], invasive computing [17]).

4.2   Shared Memory Extensions to MPI

It is not because MPI did not address shared-memory issues in recent years that MPI cannot propose solutions for such scenarios. Indeed, MPI is primarily designed to share data between multiple MPI processes and even nodes, ensuring high performance and portability over many decades. However, as mentioned earlier, we have shown that it is no longer capable of delivering peak performance for node-local operations. In order to deal with this state of affairs, we identify two major axes of evolution for MPI: process addressing and buffer-sharing.

MPI is the programming model for spatializing computation. It acts as the *embedding* model, as most HPC simulations are initially structured around the linear ranking of MPI. However, we have seen that such addressing was not possible at the node level with full performance, encouraging nested programming models instead. In recent evolutions of MPI regarding topology support, it would be desirable to allow MPI to expose shared memory in its numbering scheme – manifesting as endpoints. Shared memory structuring becomes increasingly significant when observing converged architectures that feature differentiated computing units bound to the same memory. Similarly, this would facilitate the use of a single process per node by enabling precise addressing of remote endpoints, which may exhibit differing behavior due to node-level NUMA effects.

Another way of improvement is the support for thread-aware communication primitives. This aligns with the ownership passing proposal, enabling data exchanges between ranks without doing any copy, effectively swapping pointers [2]. Additionally, this can serve as a foundation for coordination operations between collocated ranks, implementing shared memory queues [6,18,24] for inter-thread communication or Remote Procedure Calls (RPCs) [25,29]. In fact, there is a wide range of communication operations in a shared-memory environment that MPI has overlooked and which seems relevant to us. Therefore, enabling their use at the interface level, if possible as transparently as possible, appears crucial given the performance difference we have measured. Future work on MPI sessions exposing multiple MPI contexts in the same process could be a potential avenue for this support.

4.3   Thread-Based and Shared-Address Space Approaches

One potential strategy for transforming MPI into a more favorable execution environment is translating it into alternative models. In this context, several methods have emerged to bridge the gap between MPI processes. Two notable examples are Process in Process (PiP) [14,22], which employs the `dlmopen` call, and running MPI within threads [8,15,23]. However, the applicability of these methods raises concerns about compatibility with existing codes that might not be suitable for execution in threads due to their reliance on unique global variables. To overcome these challenges, it is essential to convert global variables into thread-local storage (TLS). For instance, MPC introduces a modified compiler that offers extended TLS levels for this purpose [1]. The concept of converting processes into a shared-address space represents an indirect approach to compensate the lack of shared-memory primitives in MPI. This method provides the advantage of enabling the porting of existing codes with minimal modifications, although it requires more effort at compile time to ensure correct compilation and privatization of the programs. Other approaches, such as SMARTMAP [3] and PVAS [26], consider exposing process images that can run in shared-memory by leveraging the operating system. One advantage of this indirect approach is its native support for legacy codes that do not require evolution to leverage shared-memory approaches. However, having such support in MPI would allow for a simpler implementation, without relying on either a modified compiler or operating system.

5   Evaluating Shared-Memory Gains for MPI

To better illustrate the performance improvements obtained with shared memory in MPI, let's examine a common benchmark: the OSU bibw, which measures bidirectional bandwidth between two MPI processes. We ran this benchmark on MPC with process-based (CMA enabled), thread-based, OpenMPI with CMA support[3], and MPICH compiled with UCX while forcing CMA[4]. Figure 3 shows

---

[3] `spack install openmpi fabrics=cma`.
[4] `spack install mpich netmod=ucx ^ucx +cma` and `export UCX_TLS=sm`.

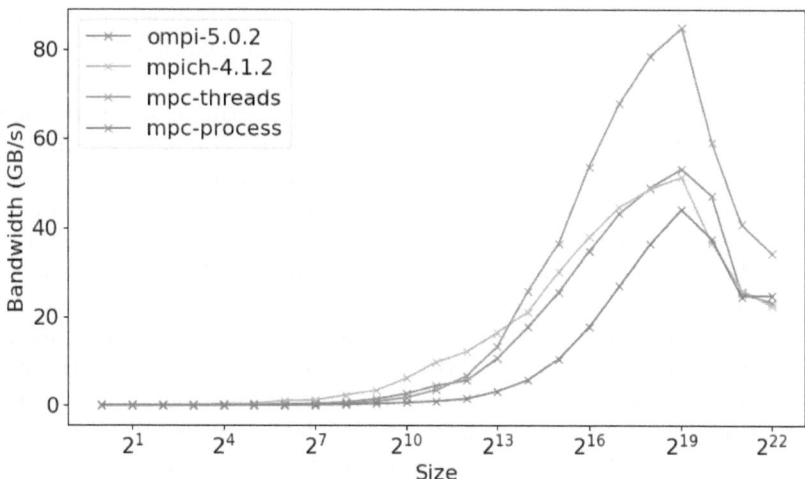

Fig. 3. Comparison of OSU Bi-Bandwidth benchmark performance between MPC other MPIs on the Intel Sapphire Rapids 4410T.

a performance improvement of 59% between MPC and OpenMPI, aligning with the expected gain of 67% for small messages inside a socket indicated in Table 1. This improvement may be put into perspective because of the added overhead of locking and MPI semantics management. For smaller sizes, MPC incurs higher overheads due to its always-on thread-based nature, but it still manages to utilize shared memory bandwidth for larger messages unlike other MPI implementations. It is important to note that XMPEM would have alleviated this observation, allowing for improved bandwidth, but it is less portable and requires a modified kernel. In contrast, shared memory is a more common solution.

Overall, through a set of relatively simple measurements utilizing common and widely accessible interfaces, we have shown that extensions to MPI enabling shared memory present an appealing approach for maintaining the advantages of both thread-based and process-based MPI approaches. In general, standard MPI (both SHM and CMA) is incapable of fully exploiting the bandwidth in a shared-memory system. On the other hand, blending models introduces complexity to programs and may restrict them to either proprietary or non-portable shared-memory runtimes. Therefore, permitting MPI to address shared-memory locality would allow a more precise division of labor between shared-memory models while leveraging the widespread and portable nature of MPI.

6   Conclusion

In this study, we examined the limitations of data transfer performance between shared memory and across processes, particularly within the context of MPI. Our investigation revealed that MPI's current model of mapping processes to

UNIX ones creates a barrier that hampers efficient data transfers within nodes. This prompted us to explore alternative approaches for adapting MPI to shared-memory environments.

Three potential solutions were investigated: the existing model with one process per node, thread-based MPI with its associated complexities and possible locking overheads, and rethinking the nature of MPI processes to expose a node-level communication layer in shared memory contexts. We concluded that the latter approach offers the most promising extension to MPI, enhancing programmability in converged architectures by allowing locality and communication within processes to be expressed transitively with respect to existing codebases.

This conclusion is supported by our findings that demonstrate integrating shared memory support into MPI can significantly enhance performance, address locality issues, and enable a more accurate division of labor between shared-memory models. These benefits include the full utilization of bandwidth in shared-memory systems, ensuring compatibility with existing codes, and providing significant performance improvements while maintaining wide system and application compatibility.

7   Future Work

In this study, our objective is to delve into shared-memory extensions for MPI. Specifically, we believe that the Session model has the potential to allow us to expose endpoints in a transparent manner within MPI. The context nesting facilitated by sessions enables us to generate endpoints by dynamically assigning ranks to all local threads participating in the `MPI_Comm_create_from_group` collective call. With a dedicated *pset*, MPI could operate in shared-memory without requiring any modifications. However, it is likely that runtimes and associated MPI calls would need tuning to fully leverage this new configuration. Under such circumstances, all RDMAs would become memcpys, message transfers would also be handled as memcpys, and both the source and destination could initiate the copy. Ultimately, on these shared-memory communicators, pointers to data could be exchanged directly rather than systematically copying.

References

1. Besnard, J.B., et al.: Introducing task-containers as an alternative to runtime-stacking. In: Proceedings of the 23rd European MPI Users' Group Meeting, pp. 51–63 (2016)
2. Besnard, J., Malony, A.D., Shende, S., Pérache, M., Carribault, P., Jaeger, J.: An MPI halo-cell implementation for zero-copy abstraction. In: Dongarra, J.J., Denis, A., Goglin, B., Jeannot, E., Mercier, G. (eds.) Proceedings of the 22nd European MPI Users' Group Meeting, EuroMPI 2015, Bordeaux, France, 21–23 September 2015, pp. 3:1–3:9. ACM (2015). https://doi.org/10.1145/2802658.2802669
3. Brightwell, R., Pedretti, K., Hudson, T.: SMARTMAP: operating system support for efficient data sharing among processes on a multi-core processor. In: SC 2008: Proceedings of the 2008 ACM/IEEE Conference on Supercomputing. IEEE (2008)

4. Buntinas, D., Mercier, G., Gropp, W.: Implementation and evaluation of shared-memory communication and synchronization operations in MPICH2 using the nemesis communication subsystem. Parallel Comput. **33**(9), 634–644 (2007)
5. Chen, C.C., et al.: MPI-xCCL: a portable MPI library over collective communication libraries for various accelerators. In: Proceedings of the SC'23 Workshops of The International Conference on High Performance Computing, Network, Storage, and Analysis, pp. 847–854 (2023)
6. Dilley, N., Lange, J.: An empirical study of messaging passing concurrency in Go projects. In: 2019 IEEE 26th International Conference on Software Analysis, Evolution and Reengineering (SANER), pp. 377–387. IEEE (2019)
7. Dosanjh, M.G., et al.: Implementation and evaluation of MPI 4.0 partitioned communication libraries. Parallel Comput. **108**, 102827 (2021)
8. Friedley, A., Bronevetsky, G., Hoefler, T., Lumsdaine, A.: Hybrid MPI: efficient message passing for multi-core systems. In: Proceedings of the International Conference on High Performance Computing, Networking, Storage and Analysis, pp. 1–11 (2013)
9. Gillis, T., Raffenetti, K., Zhou, H., Guo, Y., Thakur, R.: Quantifying the performance benefits of partitioned communication in MPI. In: Proceedings of the 52nd International Conference on Parallel Processing, pp. 285–294 (2023)
10. Goglin, B., Moreaud, S.: KNEM: a generic and scalable kernel-assisted intra-node MPI communication framework. J. Parallel Distributed Comput. **73**(2), 176–188 (2013)
11. Grant, R.E., Dosanjh, M.G.F., Levenhagen, M.J., Brightwell, R., Skjellum, A.: Finepoints: partitioned multithreaded MPI communication. In: Weiland, M., Juckeland, G., Trinitis, C., Sadayappan, P. (eds.) ISC High Performance 2019. LNCS, vol. 11501, pp. 330–350. Springer, Cham (2019). https://doi.org/10.1007/978-3-030-20656-7_17
12. Hoefler, T., et al.: MPI+ MPI: a new hybrid approach to parallel programming with MPI plus shared memory. Computing **95**, 1121–1136 (2013)
13. Hori, A., Ouyang, K., Gerofi, B., Ishikawa, Y.: On the difference between shared memory and shared address space in HPC communication. In: Panda, D.K., Sullivan, M. (eds.) SCFA 2022. LNCS, vol. 13214, pp. 59–78. Springer, Cham (2022). https://doi.org/10.1007/978-3-031-10419-0_5
14. Hori, A., et al.: Process-in-process: techniques for practical address-space sharing. In: Proceedings of the 27th International Symposium on High-Performance Parallel and Distributed Computing, pp. 131–143 (2018)
15. Huang, C., Lawlor, O., Kalé, L.V.: Adaptive MPI. In: Rauchwerger, L. (ed.) LCPC 2003. LNCS, vol. 2958, pp. 306–322. Springer, Heidelberg (2004). https://doi.org/10.1007/978-3-540-24644-2_20
16. Jin, H.W., Sur, S., Chai, L., Panda, D.K.: LiMIC: support for high-performance MPI intra-node communication on Linux cluster. In: 2005 International Conference on Parallel Processing (ICPP 2005), pp. 184–191. IEEE (2005)
17. John, J., Narvaez, S., Gerndt, M.: Invasive computing for power corridor management. Parallel Comput. Technol. Trends **36**, 386 (2020)
18. Malony, A.D., Reed, D.A., McGuire, P.J.: MPF: a portable message passing facility for shared memory multiprocessors. Technical report (1987)
19. Martinelli, A.R., Torquati, M., Aldinucci, M., Colonnelli, I., Cantalupo, B.: CAPIO: a middleware for transparent I/O streaming in data-intensive workflows. In: 2023 IEEE 30th International Conference on High Performance Computing, Data, and Analytics (HiPC), pp. 153–163. IEEE (2023)

20. MPI Forum: MPI Endpoints Proposal (2015). https://github.com/MPI-forum/ MPI-issues/issues/56. Accessed 2024
21. MPI Forum (2016): Arecv/Fsend Proposal. https://github.com/MPI-forum/MPI-issues/issues/32. Accessed 2024
22. Ouyang, K., Si, M., Hori, A., Chen, Z., Balaji, P.: CAB-MPI: exploring interprocess work-stealing towards balanced MPI communication. In: SC20: International Conference for High Performance Computing, Networking, Storage and Analysis. IEEE (2020)
23. Pérache, M., Jourdren, H., Namyst, R.: MPC: a unified parallel runtime for clusters of NUMA machines. In: Luque, E., Margalef, T., Benítez, D. (eds.) Euro-Par 2008. LNCS, vol. 5168, pp. 78–88. Springer, Heidelberg (2008). https://doi.org/10.1007/ 978-3-540-85451-7_9
24. Pieper, R., Löff, J., Hoffmann, R.B., Griebler, D., Fernandes, L.G.: High-level and efficient structured stream parallelism for rust on multi-cores. J. Comput. Lang. **65**, 101054 (2021)
25. Ross, R.B., et al.: Mochi: composing data services for high-performance computing environments. J. Comput. Sci. Technol. **35**, 121–144 (2020)
26. Shimada, A., Gerofi, B., Hori, A., Ishikawa, Y.: Proposing a new task model towards many-core architecture. In: Proceedings of the First International Workshop on Many-Core Embedded Systems, pp. 45–48 (2013)
27. Shimosaka, T., Murai, H., Sato, M.: A design of a communication library between multiple sets of MPI processes for MPMD. In: 2014 IEEE 17th International Conference on Computational Science and Engineering, pp. 1886–1893. IEEE (2014)
28. Trott, C.R., et al.: Kokkos 3: programming model extensions for the exascale era. IEEE Trans. Parallel Distrib. Syst. **33**(4), 805–817 (2021)
29. Vef, M.A., et al.: GekkoFS-a temporary distributed file system for HPC applications. In: 2018 IEEE International Conference on Cluster Computing (CLUSTER), pp. 319–324. IEEE (2018)
30. Venkata, M.G., Graham, R.L., Hjelm, N.T., Gutierrez, S.K.: Open MPI for cray XE/XK systems. In: Proceedings of the 2012 Cray User Group, Greengineering the Future, Stuttgart, Germany (2012)
31. Vienne, J.: Benefits of cross memory attach for MPI libraries on HPC clusters. In: Proceedings of the 2014 Annual Conference on Extreme Science and Engineering Discovery Environment, pp. 1–6 (2014)
32. Weingram, A., Li, Y., Qi, H., Ng, D., Dai, L., Lu, X.: xCCL: a survey of industry-led collective communication libraries for deep learning. J. Comput. Sci. Technol. **38**(1), 166–195 (2023)

MPI Ecosystem

Dynamic Resource Management for In-Situ Techniques Using MPI-Sessions

Yi Ju[1]([✉]), Dominik Huber[2], Adalberto Perez[4], Philipp Ulbl[5],
Stefano Markidis[4], Philipp Schlatter[4,6], Martin Schulz[2], Martin Schreiber[2,3],
and Erwin Laure[1]

[1] Max Planck Computing and Data Facility, 85748 Garching, Germany
{yi.ju,erwin.laure}@mpcdf.mpg.de
[2] Technical University Munich, 85748 Garching, Germany
domi.huber@tum.de, schulzm@in.tum.de
[3] Université Grenoble Alpes, 38400 Grenoble, France
martin.schreiber@univ-grenoble-alpes.fr
[4] KTH Royal Institute of Technology, 11428 Stockholm, Sweden
{adperez,markidis,pschlatter}@kth.se, philipp.schlatter@fau.de
[5] Max-Planck-Institut fur Plasmaphysik, 85748 Garching, Germany
philipp.ulbl@ipp.mpg.de
[6] Friedrich-Alexander-Universitaet Erlangen-Nürnberg, 91054 Erlangen, Germany

Abstract. The computational power of High-Performance Computing (HPC) systems increases continuously and rapidly. Data-intensive applications are designed to leverage the high computational capacity of HPC resources and typically generate a large amount of data for traditional post-processing data analytics. However, the HPC systems' in-/output (IO) subsystem develops relatively slowly, and the storage capacity is limited. This could lead to limited actual performance and scientific discovery.

In-situ techniques are a partial remedy to these problems by reducing or avoiding the data flow through the IO subsystem to/from the storage. However, in current practice, asynchronous in-situ techniques with static resource management often allocate separate computing resources for executing in-situ task(s), which remain idle if no in-situ work is at hand.

In the present work, we target improving the efficiency of computing resource usage by launching and releasing necessary additional computing resources for in-situ task(s). Our approach is based on extensions for MPI Sessions that enable the required dynamic resource management. In this paper, we propose a basic and an advanced in-situ techniques with dynamic resource management enabled by MPI Sessions, their implementations on two real-world use cases, and a critical analysis of the experimental results.

Keywords: In-situ · HPC · Dynamic resource management · MPI Session

© The Author(s), under exclusive license to Springer Nature Switzerland AG 2025
C. Blaas-Schenner et al. (Eds.): EuroMPI 2024, LNCS 15267, pp. 105–120, 2025.
https://doi.org/10.1007/978-3-031-73370-3_7

1   Introduction

High-Performance Computing (HPC) applications leveraging the continuously increasing peak performance of HPC systems can benefit data-intensive research. For instance, Computational Fluid Dynamics (CFD) simulations based on computationally expensive numerical methods can use HPC systems to analyze fluid flow. HPC systems can also help to understand and predict plasma turbulence in the edge and scrape-off layer of a magnetic confinement fusion device [28]. However, the storage capacity of HPC systems is restricted and this may limit the frequency of storing results for further analysis, which could limit scientific discovery. Another negative factor is that the input/output (IO) subsystem is also developing relatively slowly compared to the computational power and thus increasingly becoming a major bottleneck limiting an application's actual performance. Conventionally, the results generated by an application are being stored via the IO subsystem to the storage on HPC systems. This data is then read back by data analysis applications, again stressing the IO subsystems. In-situ techniques can help alleviating these problems by processing data directly at their place or dedicated separate resources without writing and reading through the IO subsystem to and from the storage. Traditional in-situ techniques with static resource management can be categorized into three types depending on how the

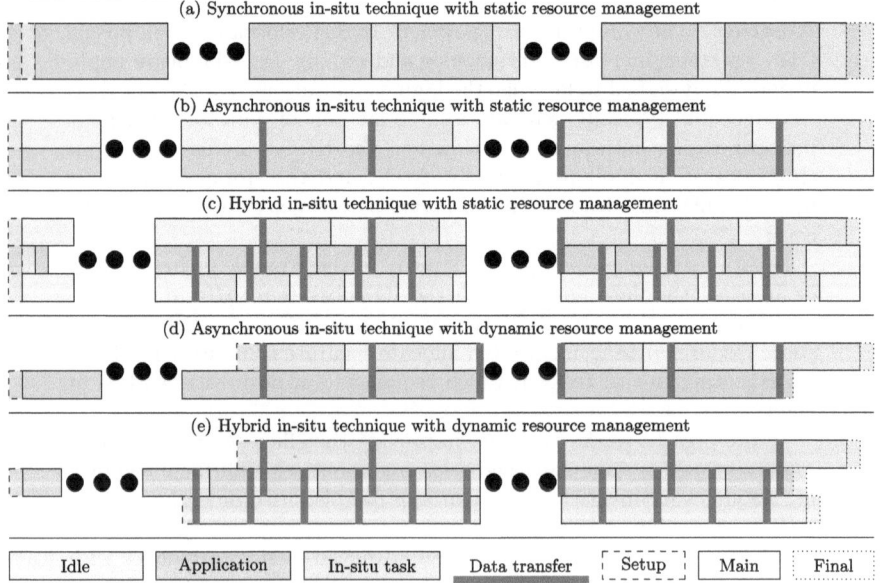

Fig. 1. Illustration of synchronous, asynchronous, and hybrid in-situ techniques with static resource management and asynchronous and hybrid in-situ techniques with dynamic resource management. Asynchronous or hybrid in-situ technique with dynamic resource management has less idle time than asynchronous or hybrid in-situ technique with static resource management

task interrupts the original application: in the *synchronous* approach (Fig. 1(a)), the in-situ task pauses the application until it has finished; in the *asynchronous* approach (Fig. 1(b)), extra resources execute the in-situ task, while the application continues its execution after having sent the data to these resources; in the *hybrid approach* (Fig. 1(c)), one part of the in-situ task pauses the original application, while separate resources execute the rest; it is thus a combination of the synchronous and asynchronous approach.

In-situ techniques can avoid or reduce the IO throughput and storage, and proper choice among the three in-situ techniques can minimize the overhead brought by the in-situ techniques. Asynchronous and hybrid in-situ techniques are typically preferred for poorly scaling in-situ task [22,23], however, they require separate resources. In many real-world scenarios, the in-situ processing will only start after a certain period, and thus, these resources may stay idle for a significant amount of time. For instance, in CFD and plasma simulation, the turbulent phase often only starts after running the simulation for many hours, and in-situ visualization will only kick in then. In such situations, the extra resources reserved for asynchronous or hybrid in-situ techniques (Fig. 1(b) and (c)) will remain idle for a significant amount of time.

With dynamic resource management, we can allocate and release additional computing resources for in-situ tasks, avoiding leaving them idle, as shown in Fig. 1(d) and (e) compared to static resource allocations as shown in Fig. 1(b) and (c). In this paper, we focus on the asynchronous and/or hybrid in-situ approaches, and thus refer to them when using the term *in-situ*, unless we explicitly specify the synchronous in-situ approach.

The introduction of MPI Sessions [15] in the MPI Standard 4.0 [27] provides a new degree of flexibility and modularity in MPI, which could make MPI more suitable for elastic in-situ workloads [9]. A recent approach [11,18,19] introduced dynamic MPI Process interface extensions for MPI Sessions and an implementation based on Open MPI [12]. In our work, we use this approach to enable MPI-based process and resource adaptivity for in-situ techniques.

We propose in-situ techniques with MPI Sessions to enable dynamic resource management, in short, dynamic in-situ techniques on HPC systems. The paper's specific contributions are:

1. A basic and advanced dynamic in-situ technique with MPI-Sessions-enabled dynamic resource management;
2. Implementations of two dynamic in-situ techniques on two real use cases;
3. A critical analysis of the dynamic asynchronous in-situ techniques;

The subsequent part of the paper is organized as follows: Sect. 2 contains a summary of related work on in-situ techniques and dynamic resource management; Sect. 3 introduces the workflow and technical details of dynamic in-situ techniques; Sect. 4 introduces the selected experimental setups and resource utilization of the dynamic in-situ techniques implemented on two real-world use cases; Sect. 5 provides a summary and discussion.

2 Related Work

In-situ visualization is one of the most common in-situ tasks. Usually, these in-situ visualization systems are being developed based on the Visualization Toolkit (VTK) data format [33], with tools like VisIt with Libsim [6,24], ParaView with Catalyst [4] and SENSEI [5]. As the name suggested, VTK focuses mainly on visualization but might require a deep copy.

ADIOS [14,25], a higher-level IO abstraction, also provides functionalities for in-situ processing. In addition to the VTK support, ADIOS/ADIOS2 also supports various data formats, facilitating the in-situ techniques. Therefore, we use the ADIOS2 library for data transfer.

Gainaru et al. [13] used the total cost in node hours to study the impact of data staging in in-situ techniques. However, their study is only based on theoretical performance models, which could not represent the performance of real-world HPC applications and in-situ tasks. Adaptivity for in-situ analysis and visualization is an active research topic and has been addressed in several other publications. *Jin et al.* [21] evaluated the benefits of dynamic resource assignments as part of a larger framework for staging-based coupled scientific workflows. According to *Dorier et al.* [9] the resource adaptivity was emulated using subsets of the static, global MPI_COMM_WORLD. *Dorier et al.* [10], describe the challenges of enabling adaptive in-situ analysis and visualization. They determined process adaptivity to be one of the main challenges, especially due to the static resource model of MPI. In a later publication [9], *Dorier et al.* used the Colza library [8], which replaced MPI with a custom communication layer to enable dynamicity due to MPI's inflexibility. Moreover, they focus on VTK-based visualization and data analysis. *Wang et al.* [35] combined Mocha [31] with Colza [8] to enable adaptive in-situ visualization without relying on MPI-based process adaptivity. They focus on visualization and propose a performance-model-based policy for resource management. Our dynamic in-situ approaches are designed for all in-situ data analysis, and the advanced approach requires no knowledge of the performance of the in-situ task. Moreover, we are using MPI-based process adaptivity.

Several approaches for enabling dynamic resource and process management in MPI have been proposed over the last two decades. DMRlib [20] is a high-level API that facilitates the adoption of dynamicity in HPC codes. It is used for dynamicity for the Conjugate Gradient solver, the Jacobi method, the N-body problem, and the bioinformatics HPG-aligner tool. ReShape [34] provides a runtime framework for malleable, iterative MPI applications that uses the collection of performance data at runtime to guide reconfiguration decisions. It has been successfully applied to LU Factorization and 2D Fast Fourier Transform codes. FLEX-MPI [26] is similar to ReShape in that it uses monitoring for the reconfiguration of malleable, iterative workloads. However, it uses a more sophisticated performance modeling approach also supporting irregular computational patterns. It has been used with applications such as Conjugate Gradient and Jacobi codes as well as EpiGraph. Elastic MPI [7] is an extended MPI implementation supporting system-driven reconfiguration of MPI applications. It was e.g. used for an AMR-based tsunami simulation introduced in [32]. AMPI [16] is an MPI implementation on top of Charm++. It differs from other approaches by using over-decomposition and migratable objects for adaptivity. It was, for instance, used to enable dynamic reconfiguration in LeanMD and Quadflow. While these approaches are suitable for monolithic, iterative workloads, applying them to more modular use cases such as in-situ analysis is challenging due to global synchronization requirements and lack of modularity imposed by the MPI World model with its embedded global MPI_COMM_WORLD communicator. In our work, we explore the potential of MPI Sessions for dynamic in-situ techniques as an alternative to the MPI World model as it provides more flexibility and modularity for dynamic process changes. In particular, we focus on the DPP approach [18], as it targets covering all different kinds of dynamic resource patterns of HPC applications including dynamic in-situ techniques.

3   Methodology

In this section, we discuss two dynamic in-situ techniques. The first one is basic and straightforward but needs systematic tests or performance models to request sufficient resources for the in-situ task. The second one is more advanced and automatically launches sufficient resources without performance models by requesting multiple times a small group of resources.

3.1   Dynamic In-Situ Techniques

For the sake of simplicity, we first assume that we have infinite resources, i.e., the in-situ task could get the required resources immediately. Figure 2 illustrates the workflow of the basic dynamic in-situ approach. When the original application reaches the first step to execute the in-situ task, it requests additional computing resources for the in-situ task. In complex simulations, this phase could take a very long time. For instance, in the plasma simulation GENE-X [28], 1.0 ms of real-time took 2.5 MCPUh on 256 Intel Skylake nodes [2]. One can see that turbulence starts at 0.2 ms, hence, it would take about two days for 256 Intel Skylake nodes to reach the turbulent state [29]. Thus, it is beneficial to ask for additional resources only when we reach the turbulent state and once these resources have been obtained, the data required for the in-situ task are sent to them, the in-situ task is being executed, and the simulation continues its iterations.

This basic dynamic in-situ technique requires the user to decide on the number of resources allocated to the in-situ task, which typically requires systematic tests to obtain a good resource estimate and/or the use of complex performance models. Our advanced in-situ dynamic technique (Fig. 3) avoids this. Instead of the user specifying the additional resources, the program automatically asks for a small group of resources and uses them for the first step of the in-situ task. This is typically one node in our implementation, as the prototype of the MPI Sessions extensions we use for the process dynamicity currently only allows new

110   Y. Ju et al.

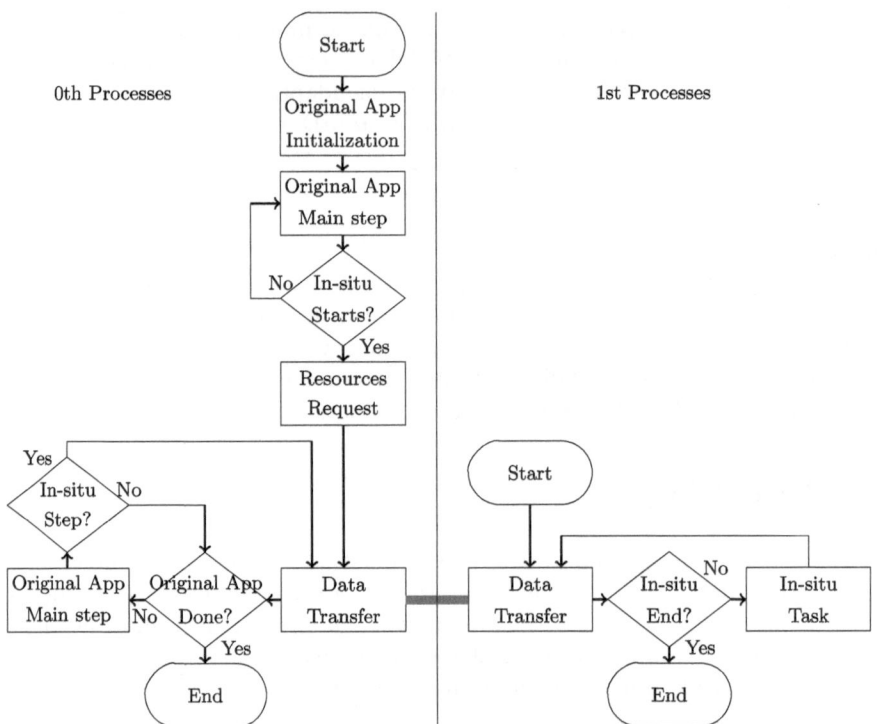

Fig. 2. The workflow of the basic dynamic in-situ technique. The figure depicts when the original application processes (the left half) request new resources for the in-situ task (the right half) and how the original application (the left half) and the in-situ task (the right half) interact in the basic dynamic in-situ technique.

MPI processes to be launched on new nodes. We therefore launch sufficient MPI processes to use the whole new node. When the second step of the in-situ task needs to be executed, the application checks if the in-situ task has finished and its resources can be used again. If this is not the case, another group of resources is allocated and used for the second in-situ step. This is repeated every time an in-situ task should be started; thus, the set of resources is growing dynamically, if necessary.

3.2   Implementation Using MPI Sessions and DPP

To achieve the required process dynamicity we used the Dynamic Processes with Process Sets (DPP) approach [18]. DPP is a set of generic design principles to enable dynamic resource management of high-performance parallel programming models such as MPI. It uses a co-design approach to provide the flexibility for application developers to express specific, dynamic resource requirements of applications while allowing the resource management software to optimize the resource utilization of the HPC system. DPP abstracts access to resources via

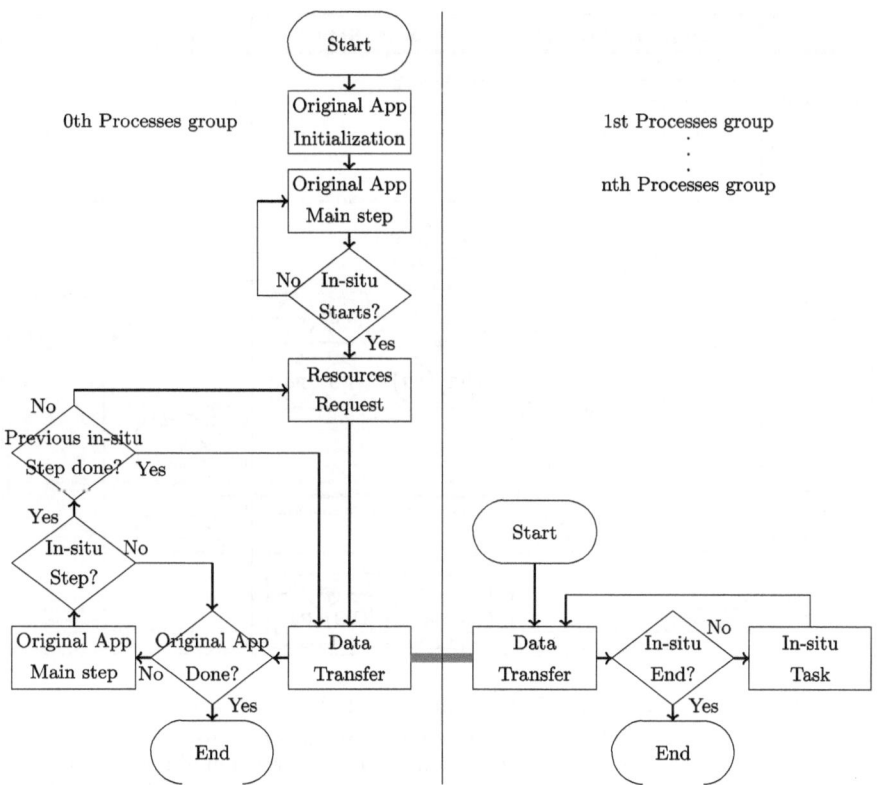

Fig. 3. The workflow of the advanced dynamic in-situ technique. The figure depicts when the original application processes (the left half) request new resources for the in-situ task (the right half) and how the original application (the left half) and the in-situ task (the right half) interact in the advanced dynamic in-situ technique.

process sets (PSets), and resource (re-)assignments as *process set operations*, leading to a *graph-based* description of the applications' resource assignments.

We used a prototype implementation [17] of the DPP approach based on Open-MPI, which provides an extended MPI Sessions interface for dynamic resources. The prototype adds two basic functionalities to the MPI Sessions routines defined in the MPI Standard 4.0. First, routines for interacting with the resource manager by sending and querying *process set operations* which express resource reconfigurations. Second, routines to access a *global dictionary* where key-value pairs can be associated with a particular process set (PSet) URI for sharing application-specific information across PSets. For brevity, we refer the reader to [18] for a more detailed description of the interface extensions.

Figure 4 illustrates the usage of this extended MPI Sessions interface during the different phases of the program flow of the dynamic in-situ approaches. The left column represents the processes of the original application, the right column

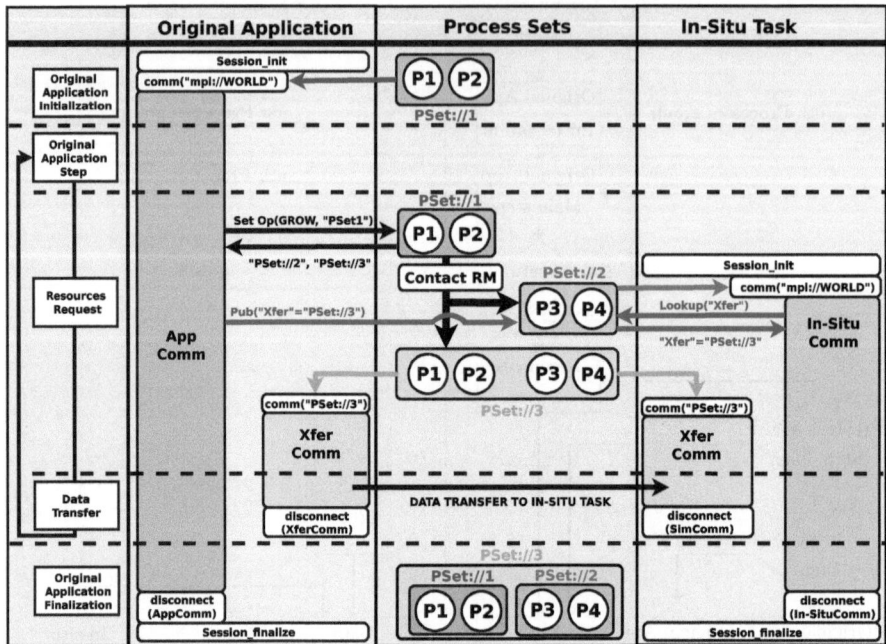

Fig. 4. Illustration of using MPI Sessions and the DPP approach to enable dynamic resources for the basic and advanced dynamic in-situ approaches. The figure depicts how the original application processes (left column) and the processes of the in-situ task (right column) use process sets and set operations (middle column) for dynamic process management and communicator creation throughout the different phases of the dynamic in-situ workflows.

represents the processes of the in-situ task(s), and the middle column shows the associated MPI process sets.

Original Application Initialization: The original application processes are started with the mpirun command (2 processes in this example). After initializing an MPI Session, the processes create a common MPI communicator for the original application using the "mpi://WORLD" URI. Note that "mpi://WORLD" is a local alias for the URI "PSet://1" containing the original application processes {p1, p2}. This is the MPI Session equivalent of using MPI_COMM_WORLD in the MPI World model. Subsequently, the original application uses this created communicator for the communication during the *Original Application Steps*.

Resources Request: If additional resources are required, the resource manager is contacted via the extended MPI Sessions interface. To this end, an MPI PSet operation of type *GROW* is specified, where the URI "PSet://1" is the input to the operation (black arrows in Fig. 4). The resource manager considers the specified process set operation in its scheduling algorithm and will eventually apply the advocated PSet operation by creating the two output PSets with URIs

"PSet://2" and "PSet://3". These URIs are returned to the original application processes.

"PSet://2" refers to the newly created processes {p3, p4} (possibly on added resources) while "PSet://3" refers to the union of "PSet://1" and "PSet://2". The newly created processes initialize an MPI Session and create a communicator for the in-situ task from the "mpi://WORLD" URI. Note, that here "mpi://WORLD" is a local alias for "PSet://2" containing processes {p3, p4}. This is similar to the disjoint MPI_COMM_WORLD communicators when using MPI_Comm_spawn. Processes can determine if they were launched dynamically via the MPI info object associated with "mpi://WORLD".

To establish communication with the original processes a common communicator has to be created from "PSet://3". To this end, the original processes publish the URI "PSet://3" in the global dictionary associated with "PSet://2", where the dynamically added processes can look up this information and participate in the communicator construction (purple arrows in Fig. 4). This common communicator can then be used for the *Data Transfer* from the original application to the in-situ task, e.g. after each application step.

Application Finalization: To terminate application processes, these processes must disconnect from all communicators they are part of before finalizing the MPI Session. While MPI_Comm_disconnect is a collective and potentially synchronizing call on the processes within the communicator, MPI_Session_finalize is a local function.

Therefore, the original application processes and the in-situ task processes can terminate independently. In this case, an MPI PSet operation of type *SUB* could be specified for a given PSet URI to release the resources associated with this PSet. However, in our implementation, we did not release resources prematurely, as the original application and in-situ tasks terminate almost simultaneously.

4 Evaluation

In this section, we present our evaluation of basic and advanced dynamic in-situ techniques. We applied them to two simulation codes with visualization as an in-situ task and compared their total execution time and resource utilization with the static in-situ synchronous and asynchronous techniques.

All the experiments are performed on the Raven supercomputer at the Max Planck Computing and Data Facility (MPCDF) [3]. One CPU node contains two Intel Xeon IceLake-SP 8360Y processors, each with 36 cores and 256 GB RAM. We repeated the same experiments three times and only reported the average here because of negligible differences among different runs. Dynamic Resource Management on HPC systems necessitates new optimization algorithms for global (dynamic) scheduling which is an active research area beyond the scope of our work. Since current production-level resource managers such as Slurm do not yet support dynamic scheduling we reserved enough resources for the original application and the in-situ task. Then, the application is started

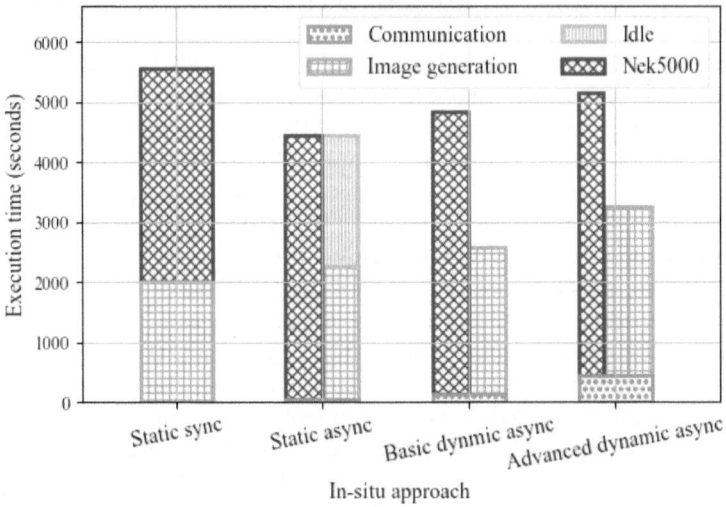

Fig. 5. Execution time of Nek5000 with in-situ image generation. The static synchronous approach (most left bars) has no communication or idle time; the static asynchronous approach (middle left bars) separates the resources into two parts from the beginning; the dynamic basic asynchronous approach (middle right bars) dynamically launches additional resources for the in-situ task; the dynamic advanced asynchronous approach (most right bars) dynamically launches two small groups of resources for the in-situ tasks.

with less than the reserved resources, requesting in-situ resources dynamically over its runtime. We compute the resource usage c using

$$c = \sum_{i}^{m} n_i \times t_i \tag{1}$$

with n_i the occupied computing nodes, their respective occupancy times t_i and m is the number of process groups. For our tests, we assume that resources are immediately available. While this might not always be the case on HPC systems with dynamic scheduling policies, our evaluation provides a basis for understanding the performance behavior of dynamic in-situ techniques.

4.1 Nek5000 with In-Situ Image Generation

The first simulation code we used is Nek5000 [1], which is a spectral element method (SEM) based CFD MPI code with excellent scalability [30]. We simulated the turbulent flow in a bent pipe and integrated the visualization with Paraview/Catalyst as the in-situ task. For the data transfer, we used a modified version of the ADIOS2 library [14]. The changes were necessary since in the original implementation of the ADIOS2 "InsituMPI" engine, MPI_COMM_WORLD is used, which does not exist in the MPI Sessions approach.

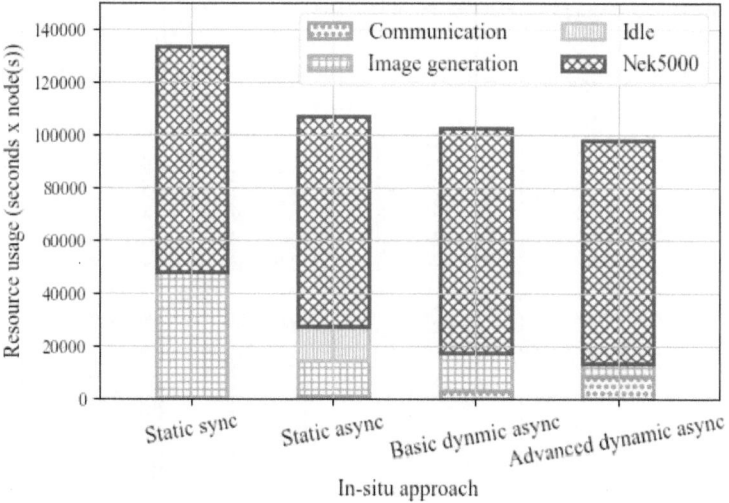

Fig. 6. Resource usage of Nek5000 with in-situ image generation. The static synchronous approach (most left bars) has no communication or idle resources; the static asynchronous approach (middle left bars) has idle resources; the dynamic basic asynchronous (middle right bars) and the dynamic advanced asynchronous (most right bars) approaches have no idle resources and the advanced approach requires fewer resources for the in-situ executions.

We executed in total 2000 simulation steps. Starting from the 1000th step, we performed one in-situ image generation every two simulation steps. For the static synchronous and asynchronous in-situ approaches, we used 24 nodes with 72 cores per node. From our tests, we determined that the static asynchronous in-situ approach has the shortest total execution time when 75% of the cores on one node are assigned to the simulation, while the rest are assigned to the in-situ image generation. Therefore, we used this ratio in our basic dynamic asynchronous in-situ approach, i.e., we started the simulation with 18 nodes and added six additional nodes for the in-situ task when image generation should start. For the advanced dynamic, asynchronous in-situ approach, we started the simulation with 18 nodes, and the simulation automatically added two times half of the node for the in-situ task.

It can be observed that our dynamic asynchronous approaches outperform the static synchronous approach in Fig. 5, although the static asynchronous approach has the best performance. The latter was expected, since in this approach the Nek5000 simulation and the image generation are allocated on the same node, therefore, their communication is faster due to the higher bandwidth for the on-node communication. For the dynamic approaches, the Nek5000 simulation must send the data to the in-situ image generation executed on other nodes, which are added with dynamic resource management. The communication time

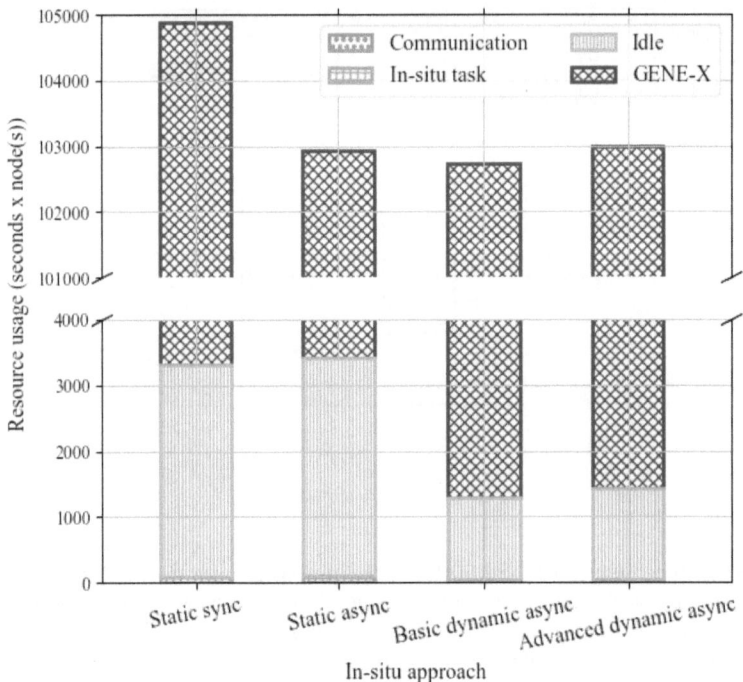

Fig. 7. Resource usage of GENE-X with in-situ image generation. The resource utilization for communication and in-situ tasks is barely visible and the dynamic asynchronous approaches (right two bars) have fewer resources idle

in the advanced dynamic approach takes longer than the basic dynamic approach because fewer cores are used for image generation and, therefore, less parallelization in the data transfer, i.e., each of them needs to collect more data from more simulation cores. In all approaches, the image generation takes almost the same time regardless of the resources because it has poor scalability.

Figure 6 shows the resource usage of the in-situ approaches. The asynchronous approaches have all a lower resource usage because fewer resources are used for parallel inefficient image generation. The resource usage for Nek5000 is dominant and unchanged because of its almost ideal scalability. With dynamic resource management, idle nodes are avoided. Our advanced dynamic approach further improves the image generation cost compared to the basic dynamic approach, while it does not need any performance test before execution.

4.2 GENE-X with In-Situ Temperature Calculations and Image Generation

The second simulation code we used is GENE-X [28], which is a 5D grid-based plasma turbulence simulation code with MPI openMP hybrid parallelization.

The in-situ task consists of two parts: 1. We calculated the 3D temperature field from the 5D space-velocity distribution function and visualized it. 2. We also used the modified ADIOS2 library for the data transfer and Paraview/Catalyst for image generation.

We executed a total of 200 simulation steps. From the 100th time step on, we performed one in-situ image generation every simulation step. We used four nodes for the static synchronous and asynchronous in-situ approaches. We used two MPI processes on each node with 36 OpenMP threads per MPI process for the static synchronous approach. For the static asynchronous in-situ approach, we specified a CPU ID binding mask for each MPI process to correctly pin the threads to the process. It has the shortest total execution time in our tests with the following configuration: two cores on each node are assigned to the two in-situ MPI processes, while the rest are to the simulation (two MPI processes and 35 cores per MPI process). Since image generation is not a large task, we started the simulation with four nodes and added one additional node for the in-situ task in the basic dynamic approach. For the advanced dynamic approach, we started the simulation with four nodes, and the simulation automatically added one additional node for the in-situ task.

As shown in Fig. 7, although the basic dynamic asynchronous approach avoids leaving the MPI process waiting for 100 simulation steps, it takes only a slightly shorter time than the static asynchronous approach, because the image generation is computationally cheaper than the simulation. The static asynchronous approach only uses two cores per node for image generation and avoids idle cores during image generation; the static synchronous approach requires no resources waiting for data, but it leaves the 35 cores per MPI processes idle when the image generation is executed; the default configuration of dynamic MPI processes added by MPI Sessions stays the same as the simulation, which leads to 35 cores per MPI process idle like the static synchronous approach. In this test case, the basic and advanced dynamic approaches use the same amount of resources. The total resource usage of the basic approach is slightly better due to a small difference in the communication time.

5   Conclusion and Discussion

In this paper, we propose two dynamic in-situ techniques on HPC systems: a basic and advanced workflow for dynamic in situ techniques. We used Nek5000 and GENE-X simulation codes as the original application and visualization with Paraview/Catalyst as the in-situ task to compare the basic and advanced dynamic in-situ approaches with static synchronous and asynchronous in-situ approaches. Although the Nek5000 with the static asynchronous in-situ image generation has the shortest execution time, the dynamic asynchronous in-situ approaches take a shorter time than the static synchronous approach. And dynamic asynchronous approaches have lower resource usage because they avoid idle time. The advanced dynamic asynchronous in-situ image generation does not need any performance model and can ask for just enough resources during runtime automatically and, therefore, has the lowest resource usage. It has

26.52% and 8.09% lower resource usage compared to the static synchronous and asynchronous in-situ approach, respectively. However, the GENE-X application shows that for the MPI and OpenMP hybrid parallelization, dynamic resource management is not effective in lowering resource usage because the new MPI process launched during runtime uses the same number of OpenMP threads per MPI process as the simulation, although the image generation has no OpenMP thread support.

In the future, we will work on dynamic in-situ techniques enabling the MPI binding of processes. This will further improve resource utilization. We also work on dynamic resource management for in-situ tasks with execution times changing in various steps, such as uncertainty quantification. For this purpose, better approaches to check the availability of the occupied resources are required. Moreover, to apply this approach to a real-world scenario on a shared computing cluster with dynamic resource management policies in place, it is necessary to consider the possibility that additional resources might not be available during the time of the request. For instance, the implementation could be extended to switch to the synchronous in-situ approach for subsequent iterations until additional resources become available or to either abandon the data transfer or output the data via the IO subsystem after compression.

Acknowledgments. This work is partially funded by the "Adaptive multi-tier intelligent data manager for Exascale (ADMIRE)" project, which is funded by the European Union's Horizon 2020 JTI-EuroHPC research and innovation program under grant Agreement number: 956748. The authors would like to express their gratitude the Max Planck Computing and Data Facility (MPCDF) for providing compute time on the Raven Supercomputer. The authors thankfully acknowledge funding from the European High-Performance Computing Joint Undertaking (JU) under grant agreement No 955701, Time-X. The JU receives support from the European Union's Horizon 2020 research and innovation programme and Belgium, France, Germany, Switzerland. Funded by the European Union. This work has received funding from the European High Performance Computing Joint Undertaking (JU) and Sweden, Finland, Germany, Greece, France, Slovenia, Spain, and Czech Republic under grant agreement No 101093261, Plasma-PEPSC.

References

1. Nek5000, a fast and scalable high-order solver for computational fluid dynamics. https://nek5000.mcs.anl.gov/
2. Supercomputer Cobra at Max Plank Computing and Data Facility. https://www.mpcdf.mpg.de/services/supercomputing/cobra
3. Supercomputer Raven at Max Plank Computing and Data Facility. https://www.mpcdf.mpg.de/services/supercomputing/raven
4. Ayachit, U., et al.: ParaView catalyst: enabling in situ data analysis and visualization. In: Proceedings of the First Workshop on In Situ Infrastructures for Enabling Extreme-Scale Analysis and Visualization, pp. 25–29 (2015)
5. Ayachit, U., et al.: The sensei generic in situ interface. In: 2016 Second Workshop on In Situ Infrastructures for Enabling Extreme-Scale Analysis and Visualization (ISAV), pp. 40–44. IEEE (2016)

6. Childs, H.: Visit: an end-user tool for visualizing and analyzing very large data (2012)
7. Compres Urena, I.A., Mo-Hellenbrand, E., Gerndt, M., Bungartz, H.J.: Infrastructure and API extensions for elastic execution of MPI applications, pp. 82–97 (2016). https://doi.org/10.1145/2966884.2966917
8. Dorier, M., Wang, Z., Ayachit, U., Snyder, S., Ross, R., Parashar, M.: Colza: enabling elastic in situ visualization for high-performance computing simulations. In: 2022 IEEE International Parallel and Distributed Processing Symposium (IPDPS), pp. 538–548. IEEE (2022)
9. Dorier, M., et al.: Towards elastic in situ analysis for high-performance computing simulations. J. Parallel Distrib. Comput. **177**, 106–116 (2023)
10. Dorier, M., Yildiz, O., Peterka, T., Ross, R.: The challenges of elastic in situ analysis and visualization. In: Proceedings of the Workshop on In Situ Infrastructures for Enabling Extreme-Scale Analysis and Visualization, ISAV 2019, pp. 23–28. Association for Computing Machinery, New York, NY, USA (2019). https://doi.org/10.1145/3364228.3364234
11. Fecht, J., Schreiber, M., Schulz, M., Pritchard, H., Holmes, D.J.: An emulation layer for dynamic resources with MPI sessions. In: Anzt, H., Bienz, A., Luszczek, P., Baboulin, M. (eds.) High Performance Computing. ISC High Performance 2022 International Workshops. ISC High Performance 2022. LNCS, vol. 13387, pp. 147–161. Springer, Cham (2022). https://doi.org/10.1007/978-3-031-23220-6_10. https://hal.archives-ouvertes.fr/hal-03856702
12. Gabriel, E., et al.: Open MPI: goals, concept, and design of a next generation MPI implementation. In: Kranzlmüller, D., Kacsuk, P., Dongarra, J. (eds.) EuroPVM/MPI 2004. LNCS, vol. 3241, pp. 97–104. Springer, Heidelberg (2004). https://doi.org/10.1007/978-3-540-30218-6_19
13. Gainaru, A., et al.: Understanding the impact of data staging for coupled scientific workflows. IEEE Trans. Parallel Distrib. Syst. **33**(12), 4134–4147 (2022)
14. Godoy, W.F., et al.: ADIOS 2: the adaptable input output system. A framework for high-performance data management. SoftwareX **12**, 100561 (2020)
15. Holmes, D., et al.: MPI sessions: leveraging runtime infrastructure to increase scalability of applications at exascale, pp. 121–129 (2016). https://doi.org/10.1145/2966884.2966915
16. Huang, C., Lawlor, O., Kalé, L.V.: Adaptive MPI. In: Rauchwerger, L. (ed.) LCPC 2003. LNCS, vol. 2958, pp. 306–322. Springer, Heidelberg (2004). https://doi.org/10.1007/978-3-540-24644-2_20
17. Huber, D.: Prototype (2023). https://gitlab.inria.fr/dynres/dyn-procs
18. Huber, D., Schreiber, M., Schulz, M., Pritchard, H., Holmes, D.: Design principles of dynamic resource management for high-performance parallel programming models (2024). https://doi.org/10.48550/arXiv.2403.17107
19. Huber, D., Streubel, M., Comprés, I., Schulz, M., Schreiber, M., Pritchard, H.: Towards dynamic resource management with MPI sessions and PMIx. In: Proceedings of the 29th European MPI Users' Group Meeting, EuroMPI/USA 2022, pp. 57–67. ACM, New York, NY, USA (2022). https://doi.org/10.1145/3555819.3555856
20. Iserte, S., Mayo, R., Quintana-Ortí, E.S., Peña, A.J.: DMRlib: easy-coding and efficient resource management for job malleability. IEEE Trans. Comput. **70**(9), 1443–1457 (2021). https://doi.org/10.1109/TC.2020.3022933
21. Jin, T., Zhang, F., Sun, Q., Romanus, M., Bui, H., Parashar, M.: Towards autonomic data management for staging-based coupled scientific workflows. J. Parallel Distrib. Comput. **146**, 35–51 (2020)

22. Ju, Y., et al.: In-situ techniques on GPU-accelerated data-intensive applications. In: 2023 IEEE 19th International Conference on e-Science (e-Science), pp. 1–10. IEEE (2023)

23. Ju, Y., Perez, A., Markidis, S., Schlatter, P., Laure, E.: Understanding the impact of synchronous, asynchronous, and hybrid in-situ techniques in computational fluid dynamics applications. In: 2022 IEEE 18th International Conference on e-Science (e-Science), pp. 295–305. IEEE (2022)

24. Kuhlen, T., Pajarola, R., Zhou, K.: Parallel in situ coupling of simulation with a fully featured visualization system. In: Proceedings of the 11th Eurographics Conference on Parallel Graphics and Visualization (EGPGV), vol. 10, pp. 101–109. Eurographics Association Aire-la-Ville, Switzerland (2011)

25. Liu, Q., et al.: Hello ADIOS: the challenges and lessons of developing leadership class I/O frameworks. Concurrency Comput. Pract. Experience **26**(7), 1453–1473 (2014)

26. Martín, G., Marinescu, M.-C., Singh, D.E., Carretero, J.: FLEX-MPI: an MPI extension for supporting dynamic load balancing on heterogeneous non-dedicated systems. In: Wolf, F., Mohr, B., an Mey, D. (eds.) Euro-Par 2013. LNCS, vol. 8097, pp. 138–149. Springer, Heidelberg (2013). https://doi.org/10.1007/978-3-642-40047-6_16

27. Message Passing Interface Forum: MPI: A Message-Passing Interface Standard Version 4.0, June 2021. https://www.mpi-forum.org/docs/mpi-4.0/mpi40-report.pdf

28. Michels, D., Stegmeir, A., Ulbl, P., Jarema, D., Jenko, F.: GENE-X: a full-f gyrokinetic turbulence code based on the flux-coordinate independent approach. Comput. Phys. Commun. **264**, 107986 (2021)

29. Michels, D., et al.: Full-f electromagnetic gyrokinetic turbulence simulations of the edge and scrape-off layer of ASDEX upgrade with GENE-X. Phys. Plasmas **29**(3) (2022)

30. Offermans, N., et al.: On the strong scaling of the spectral element solver Nek5000 on petascale systems. In: Proceedings of the Exascale Applications and Software Conference 2016, EASC 2016. Association for Computing Machinery, New York, NY, USA (2016). https://doi.org/10.1145/2938615.2938617

31. Ross, R., et al.: Mochi: composing data services for high-performance computing environments. J. Comput. Sci. Technol. **35**, 121–144 (2020). https://doi.org/10.1007/s11390-020-9802-0

32. Schreiber, M., Riesinger, C., Neckel, T., Bungartz, H.J.: Invasive compute balancing for applications with hybrid parallelization. In: 2013 25th International Symposium on Computer Architecture and High Performance Computing, pp. 136–143 (2013). https://doi.org/10.1109/SBAC-PAD.2013.20

33. Schroeder, W., Martin, K.M., Lorensen, W.E.: The Visualization Toolkit an Object-Oriented Approach to 3D Graphics. Prentice-Hall, Inc. (1998)

34. Sudarsan, R., Ribbens, C.J.: ReSHAPE: a framework for dynamic resizing and scheduling of homogeneous applications in a parallel environment. In: 2007 International Conference on Parallel Processing (ICPP 2007), p. 44. IEEE (2007)

35. Wang, Z., Dorier, M., Subedi, P., Davis, P.E., Parashar, M.: Adaptive elasticity policies for staging-based in situ visualization. Futur. Gener. Comput. Syst. **142**, 75–89 (2023)

MPI-BugBench: A Framework for Assessing MPI Correctness Tools

Tim Jammer[1]([✉])[iD], Emmanuelle Saillard[2][iD], Simon Schwitanski[3][iD],
Joachim Jenke[3][iD], Radjasouria Vinayagame[4][iD], Alexander Hück[1][iD],
and Christian Bischof[1][iD]

[1] Technical University Darmstadt, Darmstadt, Germany
{tim.jammer,alexander.hueck,christian.bischof}@tu-darmstadt.de
[2] Inria, Bordeaux, France
emmanuelle.saillard@inria.fr
[3] RWTH Aachen University, Aachen, Germany
{schwitanski,jenke}@itc.rwth-aachen.de
[4] Eviden, Bordeaux, France
radjasouria.vinayagame@eviden.com

Abstract. MPI's low-level interface is prone to errors, leading to bugs
that can remain dormant for years. MPI correctness tools can aid in writing correct code but lack a standardized benchmark for comparison. This
makes it difficult for users to choose the best tool and difficult for developers to gauge their tools' effectiveness. MPI correctness benchmarks, MPI-
CorrBench, the MPI Bugs Initiative, and RMARaceBench have emerged
to address this problem. However, comparability is hindered by having separate benchmarks, and none fully reflects real-world MPI usage
patterns. Hence, we present MPI-BugBench, a unified MPI correctness
benchmark replacing previous efforts. It addresses the shortcomings of its
predecessors by providing a single, standardized test harness for assessing
tools and incorporates a broader range of real-world MPI usage scenarios. MPI-BugBench is available at https://git-ce.rwth-aachen.de/hpc-
public/mpi-bugbench.

Keywords: MPI · Correctness · Verification · Benchmarks · Tools

1 Introduction

The Message Passing Interface (MPI, [13]) enables distributed computations in
high-performance computing (HPC). MPI, however, requires users to manually
specify details like datatypes or message tags, which is error-prone. This complexity has led to dormant bugs only uncovered after several years [1,3].

To address this issue, several MPI correctness tools have been developed
using static [1], dynamic [3,7], or a combined analysis [15] to detect issues such

---

T. Jammer, E. Saillard and S. Schwitanski—These authors contributed equally to this
research.

C. Blaas-Schenner et al. (Eds.): EuroMPI 2024, LNCS 15267, pp. 121–137, 2025.
https://doi.org/10.1007/978-3-031-73370-3_8

as process deadlocks or invalid argument values. While numerous correctness tools exist, it is difficult to compare their performance in terms of error detection capabilities objectively, implying the need for a standardized benchmark. A general evaluation framework is necessary for users to select the most suitable tool for their particular MPI usage. It allows tool developers to measure their tools' capabilities against others effectively.

As a consequence, two MPI correctness benchmarks were introduced: MPI-CorrBench (COBE, [10]) and the MPI Bugs Initiative (MBI, [9]). They offer a collection of tests, ranging from small unit tests to mini-applications and covering correct and erroneous usage of the MPI library. These tests enable the assessment of the precision of correctness tools by comparing their output against expected results. In addition, RMARaceBench (RRB, [16]) was created more recently. It is a smaller test set focused on data races of MPI one-sided communication (RMA) and other RMA programming models only.

However, separate benchmarks have created complications for both users and developers. A unified benchmark is necessary for direct comparison and evaluation. Additionally, benchmarks need to capture the diversity of real-world MPI usage, which otherwise limits their effectiveness in guiding tool development to address users' practical challenges.

To investigate the real-world relevance of the existing benchmarks, we conducted a study [4] comparing the MPI calls and their arguments present in COBE and MBI with a dataset of real-world MPI usage [5]. While neither fully represents real-world MPI usage, each benchmark has unique strengths (e.g., MBI's coverage of persistent operations and COBE's of datatypes) that complement each other.

Hence, we developed a unified correctness benchmark, MPI-BugBench, to improve tool comparability and real-world relevance. It combines the strengths of COBE, MBI, and RRB, thereby improving coverage of real-world MPI usage patterns. In summary, we make the following contributions:

- MPI-BugBench, a unified framework for consistent tool evaluation and comparison, which combines the strengths of COBE, MBI, and RRB.
- A domain-specific MPI test generator that enables the creation of tests with varying levels of error complexity, from basic misuse to granular real-world scenarios or exhaustive error combinations.
- A comprehensive evaluation of three state-of-the-art MPI correctness tools, MUST [3], ITAC [7], and PARCOACH [15], using MPI-BugBench.

The rest of the paper is structured as follows. In Sect. 2, we present existing MPI correctness benchmarks and discuss our definition of real-world MPI usage. Sect. 3 discusses our joint effort MPI-BugBench. In particular, we discuss our MPI error classification and automatic MPI test generator, and reflect on our approach's real-world MPI coverage. In Sect. 4, we evaluate three state-of-the-art MPI correctness tools using MPI-BugBench. Sect. 5 discusses limiting test code generation to real-world scenarios (as opposed to exhaustive generation) and the complications of classifying errors based on the output of correctness tools. Finally, we conclude and outline future work in Sect. 6.

2   Previous Work

In previous work [4], we evaluated COBE and MBI's real-world applicability by applying a feature-scoring method based on our previous MPI study [5] that resulted in a dataset of 96 HPC codes (henceforth called HPC dataset). Our scoring method assesses how closely the MPI usage patterns in these correctness benchmarks reflect those found in the HPC dataset. Specifically, COBE covers approximately 40% of the MPI usage observed in the HPC dataset, while MBI covers around 30%.

The relatively low scores of these benchmarks can be attributed to their creation predating our MPI study. Previous studies, e.g., [8], primarily focused on MPI function calls without considering parameter usage patterns. These patterns provide a more detailed understanding of how users interact with MPI, such as determining the most common datatypes in collective operations.

In Sect. 2.1, we provide a brief overview of the correctness benchmarks COBE, MBI, and RRB. We elaborate on our scoring algorithm in Sect. 2.2. It serves as the guideline for designing MPI-BUGBENCH's test code generator described in Sect. 3.

2.1   Correctness Benchmarks

MPI-CorrBench COBE [10] contains 510 small-scale C language tests, including 202 correct and 308 incorrect codes. In particular, the correct test cases have been extracted from an MPI library implementation test set. The incorrect codes, on the other hand, have been hand-written. Each incorrect test contains a brief description of the error. COBE also includes well-known (C/C++) HPC mini-apps where the authors manually introduced specific errors. In COBE, erroneous arguments, erroneous program flow, and mismatching arguments across communication calls are the key error types.

The MPI Bugs Initiative MBI [9] contains 1668 C language codes, including 682 correct and 986 incorrect codes. To generate these test cases, MBI uses a template engine. Templates for the various MPI categories contain placeholder tokens that get replaced by (in-)correct usage of MPI calls to generate the final test case. Each test defines a header that describes the intent of each code and specifies how to execute and evaluate it. In MBI, the errors are categorized by the scope in which they can arise: (a) single call (invalid parameter), (b) single process (resource leak, request lifecycle, and local concurrency), and (c) multi processes (parameter matching, message race, call ordering, and global concurrency).

RMARaceBench RRB [16] focuses on different data race test cases for the remote memory access (RMA) models MPI RMA, OpenSHMEM [14], and GASPI [2]. It consists of 107 different small-scale C codes targeting MPI RMA, of which 43 are correct and 64 are incorrect. Like MBI, the test cases are semi-automatically generated based on code templates, covering different combinations of RMA communication and synchronization methods. The errors are categorized into (a) local concurrency issues, i.e., a user-specified local buffer of an RMA operation is accessed before completion, (b) global concurrency issues, i.e., concurrent conflicting RMA accesses from different processes are not correctly synchronized, (c) incorrect atomicity, i.e., the atomicity semantics of MPI RMA are violated, and (d) hybrid races in combination with threading via OpenMP.

2.2   MPI Feature Usage Analysis

In a previous study [5], we developed a static code analysis toolchain that (a) extracts MPI calls and their arguments, (b) applies an MPI feature classification (closely following the MPI standard's categorization), and (c) cross-references MPI argument handles across detected function calls, Listing 1.

```
1   MPI_Datatype struct_type; // Opaque type handle
2   // Construct struct type:
3   MPI_Type_create_struct(num_members, block_length,
4                          offsets, member_types, &struct_type );
5   MPI_Type_commit( &struct_type ); // Make MPI aware of struct type
6   MPI_Send(buffer, 1, struct_type , ...);
```

Listing 1: Example of constructing a struct type. We need to consider arguments of MPI functions to deduce that the send operation uses the struct datatype.

This resulted in a dataset of MPI usage at an argument granularity for 96 real-world MPI codes. We use this dataset to assess whether the existing MPI correctness benchmarks and MPI-BUGBENCH reflects real-world MPI usage. In the following, we describe our scoring workflow for this assessment developed in our previous study [4].

Scoring MPI Usage For each MPI feature category, e.g., point-to-point (PtP) operations, we calculate a percentage representing the proportion of (real-world) MPI usage patterns that are covered by the correctness benchmark. To that end, for this MPI usage pattern scoring, we consider: (1) The MPI call, (2) the *Datatype* and *Reduction Operator*, (3) the *Count* (4) and if wildcards, such as ANY_TAG are used; (5) for collective operations, the root *Rank* is also important to the usage pattern. To be counted towards usage scoring, for each individual MPI call in the real-world dataset, the aforementioned aspects must be present in the MPI correctness benchmark.

Additionally, the score for each usage pattern is based on its frequency in our real-world dataset, as shown in Fig. 1. As the dataset contains operations with varying arguments, a 100% score requires all operations for each MPI feature category to be present with all arguments in the correctness benchmark. Consider a dataset with six scatter operations and four broadcast operations. If all six scatter operations fully match, but only one out of four broadcast operations match (e.g., one uses MPI_FLOAT and the others use MPI_DOUBLE), the score of the benchmark would be 70% for collectives. The full details of this scoring workflow are explained in [4]. The reasoning behind testing the same errors with several distinct MPI usage patterns is further detailed in Sect. 3.2.

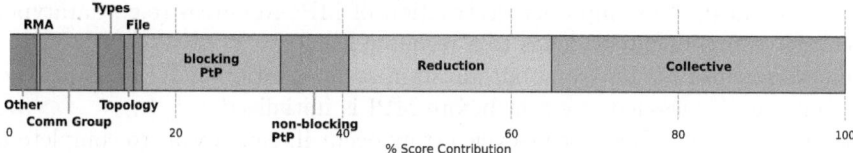

Fig. 1. Weighting of MPI categories, adapted from [4]. Collectives and reductions are predominantly used, followed by PtP operations. This indicates that correctness benchmarks should focus on these categories first to improve their scoring.

3   Design of MPI-BugBench

In the design of MPI-BugBench (MBB), we adopted and expanded upon the test code generation idea of the MPI Bugs Initiative while integrating the test cases from MPI-CorrBench (COBE) and RMARaceBench (RRB). MBB contains different unit tests with exactly one MPI usage error per test case. This allows for a more fine-grained evaluation of a correctness tool, as one can individually compare the tool's performance for specific errors. The tools are evaluated in a container-based infrastructure to ensure portability (see Section 4.2). In this section, we first discuss the different types of errors we consider in Section 3.1, while Section 3.2 discusses different instantiations of errors that can be generated. The explanation of how the test cases are generated follows in Section 3.3.

3.1   Error Types Covered

Different kinds of programming errors in MPI may lead to different (non-deterministic) failures at runtime. Both COBE and MBI provide similar classifications of such MPI programming errors. MPI-BugBench mainly adapts the classification introduced by MBI. For detailed code examples of the different error classes, we refer to COBE [10] and MBI [9].

In general, MPI errors can be categorized into three different categories:

1. **Single call errors**: These errors are only related to local MPI functions and can be detected by only analyzing the parameters of a given MPI function.
2. **Process-local errors**: These errors often consist of an inconsistency between the local context of a process and the parameters of a given MPI call in that process. Thus, the detection of these errors requires analysis of local process information.
3. **Multi-processes errors**: These errors result from the interplay of multiple application processes, such as a deadlock.

Single call errors

1. Invalid Parameters: This category contains invalid parameters in an MPI call, such as a negative value for a rank.

Process-local errors

2. Resource Leak: Any improper destruction of MPI resources (e.g., datatype, request, communicators) leads to a resource leak.
3. Initialization of MPI: Wrong initialization or finalization of MPI can lead to errors, e.g., if messages are sent before MPI is initialized.
4. Request Lifecycle: Request lifecycle errors occur if, e.g., a wait to complete a nonblocking operation is missing.
5. Local Concurrency: A local concurrency error occurs when a process accesses a memory region asynchronously read or written by MPI. This type of error is produced with nonblocking and one-sided communication. An example would be using a message buffer before the nonblocking operation completes.
6. Epoch Lifecycle: An epoch lifecycle error occurs when MPI RMA operations are wrongly synchronized by, e.g., mixing different RMA synchronization modes (fences and locks) or performing an RMA operation outside an access epoch.

Multi-processes errors

7. Message Race: Wildcard receive calls can lead to non-deterministic message matching with potential senders, possibly leading to deadlocks.
8. Parameter Matching: Parameter matching corresponds to MPI calls matched with incompatible arguments. An example is a collective operation, where the processes do not agree on a root, which can result in a deadlock.
9. Call Ordering: Wrong ordering of MPI calls can lead to a call mismatch, e.g., when all processes call a receive operation before any process calls a send operation, resulting in a deadlock.
10. Global Concurrency: Global concurrency errors occur if two or more processes access the same memory region (at least one access is a write). An example would be two concurrent `MPI_Put` operations accessing the same memory region at the target process.

3.2   Error Instantiations Covered

Apart from testing for different *kinds* of errors explained in Section 3.1, MBB also tests for different instances of the *same kind* of error. For example, a datatype mismatch between a `double` and an `integer` may result in a message size mismatch. It may be more easily spotted by a correctness checking tool than a different mismatch, resulting in the same message length (e.g., between `integer` and `unsigned integer`). Therefore, MBB can be used to assess the coverage of a tool regarding the different possible MPI errors supported and can additionally be used to assess the implementation quality regarding the reliability of finding different instances of the same type of error.

Testing for all the possible instances of an error (e.g., wrongfully matching each datatype with all other types) leads to a high combinatorial complexity. MBB can generate over four million test cases when all combinations are considered exhaustively.

Several studies like [5, 8] have shown that most applications only use a limited subset of MPI functionality. Hence, testing a tool with all possible MPI usage patterns is probably unnecessary. Furthermore, the study by Hück et al. points out that derived MPI datatypes are more commonly used in point-to-point operations than in collective operations [5].

In order to limit the number of cases generated and to facilitate a more efficient evaluation of correctness tools, MPI-BUGBENCH contains different *coverage levels* to generate different sets of test cases gradually:

1. **Basic cases**: The basic cases include only one instance of an error (e.g., one datatype mismatch).
2. **Sufficient coverage**: This level contains multiple instances of the "same" kind of error, that should be sufficient to evaluate if specific MPI errors are supported by a tool by containing multiple examples, covering all possible values for the mismatching parameters involved. In terms of datatype mismatches, for example, for each MPI datatype, at least one mismatch is included. In order to only include usage patterns that can be observed in the real world, we refine this level into 2.1 "Sufficient coverage of real-world patterns" and 2.2 "Sufficient coverage of all possible MPI usage pattern".
3. **Full Testcaseset**: The full set contains all possible instantiations of an error. In the case of datatype mismatches, all possible mismatches between all possible MPI datatypes are included. Again, this level can be refined into 3.1 "Full coverage of real-world usage patterns" and 3.2 "Full coverage of all possible MPI usage patterns" to include only usage patterns found in the real world or all theoretically possible ones.

The number of cases generated for the five levels for point-to-point, collective, and RMA operations is shown in Table 1.

In order to determine which usage patterns occur in the real world, MBB uses the data set collected by Hück et al. [5], excluding the Fortran cases, as Fortran is currently not part of MBB. MBB can also be used to generate test cases tailored to a more limited set of use cases by replacing the complete real-world data set with a different one, e.g., for one specific application.

3.3   Test Case Generation

MBB's test generation builds upon the infrastructure of the MPI Bugs Initiative and enhances it in several ways. The original test case generation infrastructure relied on text replacement. We improved it to generate a variety of test cases automatically based on test generator scripts. Each test generator is a Python

Table 1. Number of test cases per feature.

	Level 1	Level 2.1	Level 2.2	Level 3.1	Level 3.2
P2P	49	870	24,116	2,789	3,004,968
COLL	40	774	23,937	3,246	1,121,865
RMA	39	415	415	1,898	1898
Total	128	2,059	48,539	7,933	4,128,731

```
1   def generate(self, generate_level, real_world_score_table):
2     for func in mpi_send_funcs :
3       for buf_to_use in [ "NULL", 'MPI_BOTTOM', 'MPI_IN_PLACE']:
4         tm = get_send_recv_template(func, "mpi_irecv") # get a TemplateManager
5         for call in tm.get_instruction(identifier="MPICALL", return_list=True):
6           # send is executed by rank 1 in default template
7           if call.get_rank_executing() == 1:
8             call.set_arg("buf", buf_to_use) # set buffer to invalid value
9             call.set_has_error() # mark where the error is
10            # set an appropriate description for the error:
11            tm.set_description("InvalidParam-Buffer-" + func, # short description
12            "Invalid Buffer: "+buf_to_use) # long description
13            yield tm
```

Listing 2: Illustration of the test-case generation function for invalid buffer errors.

class that implements a generator function. The infrastructure will execute all applicable generators to produce the test case set. The user can target a specific MPI version or feature, with the effect of cases not fitting the user's criteria being discarded.

In particular, Listing 2 shows the generation of an invalid buffer error. In line 4, a default point-to-point template is instantiated. Then, the **generate** function needs to find the call where the buffer argument should be replaced with the invalid one. Line 5 of Listing 2 iterates over the send and receive call of the default template, while line 7 selects the send call. The **MPICall** object allows setting an invalid buffer argument (line 8). Line 9 marks the erroneous MPI call for later evaluation. The only thing left for the **generate** function is to set an appropriate error description in line 11 of Listing 2, before yielding the instantiated **TemplateManager** to the generation infrastructure. The generation infrastructure will then generate the resulting erroneous code (illustrated in Listing 3) into a file for later compilation and execution with a correctness tool. The Python yield construct turns the function into a generator. Iteratively calling the function returns different errors. In the example of Listing 2, multiple different invalid buffer argument errors are created for all flavors of MPI point-to-point send functions. The arguments to the **generate** function limit the generated instantiations of an error, as it may lead to redundancy to test for all possible circumstances where an error can occur, as explained in Section 3.2.

```
1   // Description: Invalid Buffer: NULL // header is shortened
2   int main(int argc, char **argv) {
3     // init MPI and setup rank variable
4     int *buf = (int *)calloc(10, sizeof(int));
5     if (rank == 0) {
6       MPI_Irecv(buf, 10, MPI_INT, 1, 0, MPI_COMM_WORLD, &mpi_request_0);
7       MPI_Wait(&mpi_request_0, MPI_STATUS_IGNORE); }
8     if (rank == 1) {
9       /*MBBERROR_BEGIN*/ MPI_Send(NULL, 10, MPI_INT, 0, 0,
10      MPI_COMM_WORLD); /*MBBERROR_END*/ }
11    // free and finalize
12  }
```

Listing 3: Excerpt of one error code produced by the generator shown in Listing 2.

4 Evaluation of Correctness Tools

This section first discusses the real-world coverage of the generated test cases in Section 4.1. We then evaluate three state-of-the-art MPI correctness tools using the generated test cases in Section 4.2.

4.1 Real-World Applicability

MPI-BUGBENCH'S approach vastly improves its real-world applicability when considering the coverage level 2.1, as described in Section 3.2. The real-world applicability, as explained in Section 2.2, is illustrated in Fig. 2. High coverage of the most relevant real-world usage pattern is obtained in most categories, with an overall coverage score of more than 75%. MBB has surpassed the original works of MPI-CorrBench and MPI Bugs Initiative in all categories. The current lack of coverage for the *Types* category is explained in a surprisingly high number of conversion functions like Type_f2c, which our benchmark currently does not cover as Fortran is not supported. For the other category, the lack of coverage is mostly due to MPI I/O which is currently not covered by MPI-BUGBENCH. Nevertheless, the most important aspects of real-world MPI usage are covered, which also can be seen in Table 2, where the overall coverage scores are compared between the three benchmarks.

We note that using a higher generation level of MBB does not further increase the coverage score. The reason is that the coverage score only counts if a usage pattern is included at least once. As explained in Section 3.2, the idea of coverage level 2.1 is that each usage combination is part of at least one instance of every applicable error. However, not all erroneous combinations are tested to allow for a more efficient tool evaluation.

4.2 Evaluation of Correctness Tools

We use MPI-BUGBENCH to evaluate three active MPI correctness tools relying on different techniques to detect errors: ITAC (v2021.3), MUST (v1.10.0),

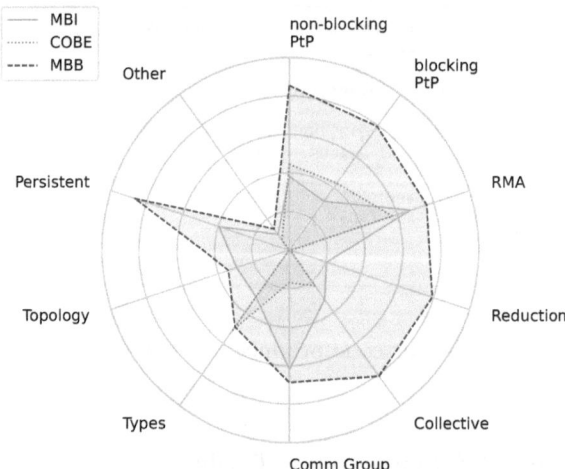

Fig. 2. Comparison of real-world applicability of MPI Correctness Benchmarks. MBI (orange) denotes the MPI Bugs Initiative. COBE (blue) denotes MPI-CorrBench. MBB (green) denotes MPI-BugBench with coverage level 2.1. We used the methodology proposed by Hück et al. [4] for evaluation, without including the Fortran codes in the real-world dataset (see Sect. 2.2). (Color figure online)

Table 2. Total real-world coverage score. The scoring is described in Section 2.2.

	Erroneous (%)	Correct (%)	Total (%)
MBB coverage level 2.1	74.94	51.15	74.97
MBB coverage level 1	28.45	19.85	28.74
COBE	25.61	47.85	51.68
MBI	28.32	28.32	28.32

and PARCOACH (v2.4.0). Intel Trace Analyzer and Collector (ITAC) [7] profiles and analyzes MPI programs to check their correctness. It intercepts MPI calls and generates trace files that can be analyzed to understand the program's behaviors. MUST [3] detects different kinds of MPI errors such as deadlocks, type mismatches, or invalid arguments during the execution. For extended type correctness checks of user-specified buffers, it relies on TypeART [6] and LLVM 14. PARCOACH [15,19] detects collective and one-sided operation misuse with a static/dynamic approach. It emits warnings for potential errors found at compile-time and verifies these potential errors during the execution of programs. PARCOACH's static analysis is based on LLVM 15. In this section, we only used the static analysis of PARCOACH.

We use coverage level 2.1 of MBB that generates roughly 2000 test codes. The experiments used the MBB infrastructure in a Docker image based on Debian 12, which contained all tool dependencies. The MUST container uses MPICH

4.0.2, the PARCOACH container uses Open MPI 4.1.4, and the ITAC container uses Intel MPI 2021.12.

Since some tests may crash or hang up in a deadlock, we specified a time-out of 120 seconds for each test execution. To speed up the overall runtime of the benchmark, the MBB infrastructure supports parallel test execution. We performed the evaluation on a cluster node with 96 cores, using a pool of 16 runners so that 16 tests could run in parallel. This leaves enough spare cores to start additional tool processes, as required by MUST. On the described setup, the execution of the tests requires 2 minutes for PARCOACH, 27 minutes for ITAC, and 58 minutes for MUST. PARCOACH is the fastest tool, as its static analysis does not execute the tests.

Result Categorization The resulting tool output of each test is classified into exactly one of the following categories:

- True Positive (TP): Error reported on an erroneous test case.
- True Negative (TN): No error reported on a correct test case.
- False Positive (FP): Error reported on a correct test case.
- False Negative (FN): No error reported on an erroneous test case.
- Compilation Error (CE): The test case could not be compiled with the tool.
- Runtime Error (RE): The tool execution on a correct test case crashed or ran into a timeout (here: 120s)

A compilation error (CE) may occur when the tool does not support all MPI calls in the test, e.g., due to an outdated MPI library compatibility. An execution is classified as runtime error (RE) when the execution on a *correct* test case crashes or runs into a timeout without any error report. If the tool falsely reports an error on a correct test case and the execution crashes or runs into a timeout, this still counts as FP. Thus, an issued error report always takes precedence for FP in the classification over a runtime error (RE). Further, an execution on an erroneous test cases is never classified as runtime error, because the test may crash or timeout itself, independently of the tool.

Tool Results Table 3 shows the results of each tool for all tests on coverage level 2.1. The first part of the table shows the aforementioned classification of test executions for the different tools. The rest of the table gives the following derived metrics, as also defined by MBI:

- Coverage $Cov = 1 - \frac{CE}{Total\ tests}$, Conclusiveness $Cc = 1 - \frac{CE+RE}{Total\ tests}$
- Specificity $S = \frac{TN}{TN+FP}$, Recall $R = \frac{TP}{TP+FN}$, Precision $P = \frac{TP}{TP+FP}$
- F1 Score $F1 = \frac{2 \cdot P \cdot R}{P+R}$, Overall Accuracy $OA = \frac{TP+TN}{Total\ tests}$

Coverage and conclusiveness demonstrate the robustness of a tool, i.e., the ability to compile and draw a diagnostic on codes. Specificity, recall, precision, and F1 score are standard metrics used to evaluate tools. Specificity measures the ability to avoid identifying errors in *correct* codes, while recall measures

Table 3. Tool evaluation against MPI-BugBench on coverage level 2.1. The best results are in bold.

Tool	Errors		Results				Robustness		Usefulness				OA
	CE	RE	TP	TN	FP	FN	Cov	Cc	S	R	P	F1	
ITAC	75	0	**1386**	**358**	13	**228**	0.96	0.964	0.95	**0.82**	**0.99**	**0.92**	**0.85**
MUST	**0**	9	1153	359	**7**	532	**1**	0.996	**0.96**	0.68	**0.99**	0.81	0.73
PARCOACH	**0**	**0**	594	271	104	1091	**1**	**1**	0.72	0.35	0.85	0.50	0.42
Ideal tool	*0*	*0*	*1685*	*375*	*0*	*0*	*1*	*1*	*1*	*1*	*1*	*1*	*1*

CE: Compilation Error, RE: Runtime Error, TP: True Positive, TN: True Negative, FP: False Positive, FN: False Negative, Cov: Coverage, Cc: Conclusiveness, S: Specificity, R: Recall, P: Precision, F1: F1 Score, OA: Overall Accuracy

the ability to find existing errors. Precision is the confidence in TN results, and F1 score is the overall bug-finding quality. Finally, overall accuracy gives the proportion of correct diagnostics for all tests when considering compilation and runtime errors. The last row of the table gives the results of an ideal tool.

PARCOACH and MUST compile all test cases and, therefore, have a coverage of 1. ITAC comes with Intel MPI that currently does not support MPI 4.0 features such as partitioned communication. Due to undefined MPI functions, this leads to compilation errors (CE) for those test cases. With MUST, 9 executions on correct tests resulted in runtime errors (RE) that are related to the internal type verification. It does not consider less frequently used data types such as `MPI_DOUBLE_INT` or `MPI_2INT` correctly. ITAC did not crash or timeout on any test. Since PARCOACH analyzes the codes only statically, it also cannot have any runtime errors.

ITAC has the best classification results of the tools, with an overall accuracy of 0.85 and an F1 score of 0.92. MUST achieves a similarly high precision of 0.99 compared to ITAC but detects fewer issues overall leading to a recall of 0.68. Still, the F1 score of MUST is 0.81. PARCOACH is focused on a small subset of errors, in particular collective operations. Thus, it returns many false negatives and has low scores for most of the metrics, resulting in an F1 score of 0.50.

Fig. 3 illustrates the tool results individually for the different MPI features. MUST and ITAC perform similarly for the P2P and Collective tests. Both tools have a larger number of false negatives (FN) because they fail to detect issues in erroneous test cases containing less frequently used MPI calls or data types. Since PARCOACH focuses on error detection in collective operations, it performs well on those tests, but falls short on the P2P tests. For the RMA test cases, MUST only detects invalid parameter errors. ITAC detects invalid parameter and additionally epoch lifecycle errors. Both tools do not detect local concurrency or global concurrency errors in RMA. Only PARCOACH detects some of the RMA local concurrency issues but also detects such issues in correct test cases, leading to some false positives (FP). An extension of MUST [17] to check for local and global concurrency errors in RMA programs has not been integrated into the current release and thus has not been tested. Similarly, PARCOACH

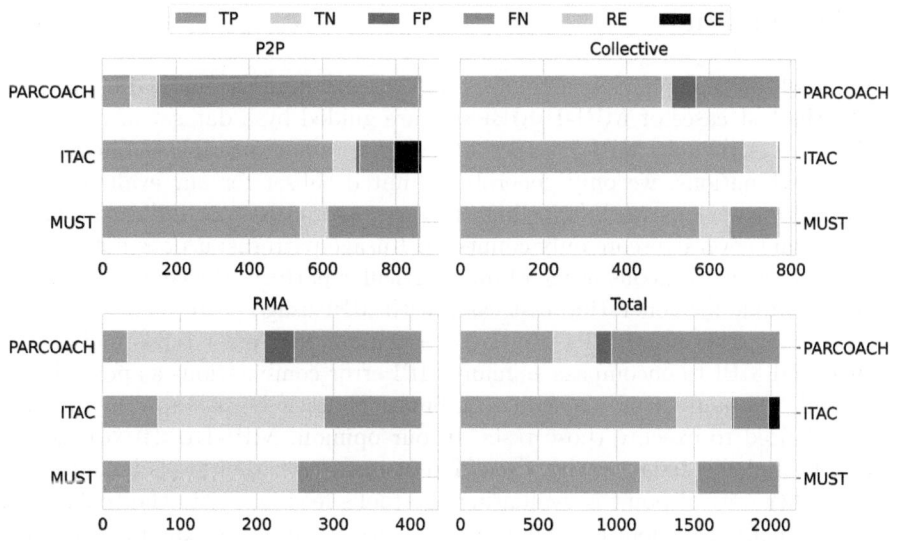

CE: Compilation Error RE: Runtime Error, TP: True Positive, TN: True Negative, FP: False Positive, FN: False Negative

Fig. 3. Tool evaluation using MPI-BugBench including a breakdown for each MPI feature category.

implements a dynamic analysis [18,19] for RMA that significantly improves the detection quality on local and global concurrency errors in RMA, but has also not been tested in our infrastructure. For both MUST and PARCOACH, we plan to integrate and incorporate those extended RMA analyses in future work.

We compared the results shown in Table 3 on coverage level 2.1 with those on coverage level 1. The derived metrics show similar results on both levels. Nevertheless utilizing level 2.1 does reveal some additional shortcomings of the tools, that cannot be uncovered by using only coverage level 1. An example are the runtime errors (RE) of MUST when utilizing less frequently used datatypes, as these runtime errors are not present, when testing MUST only with coverage level 1. As these cases are rare however, they do not significantly impact the overall scoring of the tools. This means that the tools do support a broad range of real-world usage patterns, with some errors in some rather rare cases.

Summarizing the results, the three tested state-of-the-art tools ITAC, MUST, and PARCOACH show a good coverage on real-world usage patterns. For some less frequently used MPI features, the tools sometimes do not detect errors correctly or crash. With MBB, we provide a test set that should motivate tool developers to improve their tool's classification quality by also considering corner cases that are still relevant in real-world MPI programs.

5 Discussion

Compared to the previous benchmarks COBE, MBI, and the focused benchmark RRB, the test cases of MPI-BugBench are guided by a dataset of real-world MPI usage. Although, MPI-BugBench can generate all possible erroneous MPI usage combinations, we only generate a limited subset for our evaluation. As discussed in previous work [4], a high coverage score does not indicate rigorous testing. The coverage score only counts MPI usage patterns; it does not account for the possible erroneous usage of any particular pattern. Hence, our scoring is merely a guide for generating test cases with MPI usage patterns of real-world relevancy. Furthermore, MPI-BugBench combines all error types included in COBE and MBI to encompass as many MPI error combinations as possible. To that end, the number of erroneous combinations must be balanced against the time required to execute those tests. In our opinion, MPI-BugBench is well suited to find this balance with the different test generation levels included.

Another critical point is evaluating the tool's feedback: Are the tool's error messages helpful in pointing out the root cause of an error? In this work, the evaluation discussed in Section 4.2 only checks whether the tool reported an error on a test case or not. It does not verify the usefulness of the error report. From our perspective, there are two aspects that contribute to the usefulness of a tool. First, the correct error class should be reported by the tool. For example, if a tool reports a data race on a test case that contains a deadlock, then this error report is not useful at all. Further, if the error report does not include the affected source code lines, users have to locate the root cause of the error on their own which is not applicable to larger codes. Moreover, since the tools' output is not standardized, it may be difficult to argue whether the expected error was actually discovered. Nevertheless, MBB facilitates in-depth analysis of the origin of the error by marker comments pointing to the location of the erroneous MPI usage in the generated test cases. This work focuses on how real-world usage data can guide the test cases, but we plan to add a tool's feedback analysis like in [11, 12].

6 Conclusion

In this work, we introduce MPI-BugBench, a unified benchmark for assessing MPI correctness tools. It consolidates previous efforts, offering a standardized test harness that mirrors real-world MPI usage in HPC codes. Utilizing a test code generator, MPI-BugBench creates tests with varying levels of error complexity, covering basic misuses to exhaustive error combinations. This allows for detection of bugs in the tools implementation for some more rarely used cases.

We evaluate three state-of-the-art MPI correctness tools using 2,060 generated codes. These test codes cover 75% of MPI usage patterns identified in 96 HPC codes, doubling the coverage compared to previous MPI correctness benchmarks. The test code generator produces test codes, which can be correctly compiled and run by the static and dynamic correctness tools without (unexpected) issues. The dynamic tools ITAC and MUST have a relatively high degree of real-world applicability with an overall accuracy of about 85% and 73%, respectively. PARCOACH is limited in focus and only performs well on collective operations and some RMA features. However, it has a clear advantage regarding run time, as it only utilizes static analysis without the need for the actual execution of the tests.

For future work, we plan to extend MPI-BUGBENCH with a more detailed tools report analysis to analyze the helpfulness of the error messages given by the tools, in particular the reported error type and source code lines. Although 80% of real-world usage patterns are already covered by MPI-BUGBENCH, we further want to expand the scope of our correctness benchmark suite by incorporating currently not covered MPI features such as MPI I/O. Another way to increase the scope of MPI-BUGBENCH is to include Fortran test cases. Additionally, we want to add the hybrid OpenMP+MPI errors from COBE alongside other MPI+X programming models. We also want to incorporate more complex error cases, such as nondeterministic instances of errors, that depend on the input parameters.

In summary, MPI-BUGBENCH serves as a comprehensive and unified benchmark reflecting actual MPI usage in HPC environments. The infrastructure is available at https://git-ce.rwth-aachen.de/hpc-public/mpi-bugbench.

Acknowledgments. This work was supported by the Hessian Ministry for Higher Education, Research and the Arts through the Hessian Competence Center for High-Performance Computing, and by the Federal Ministry of Education and Research (BMBF) and the states of Hesse and North Rhine-Westphalia as part of the NHR program.

Disclosure of Interests. The authors have no competing interests to declare that are relevant to the content of this article.

References

1. Droste, A., Kuhn, M., Ludwig, T.: MPI-checker: static analysis for MPI. In: Proceedings of the Second Workshop on the LLVM Compiler Infrastructure in HPC, LLVM '15, ACM (2015), https://doi.org/10.1145/2833157.2833159
2. GASPI Forum: GASPI: Global Address Space Programming Interface 17.1 (2017), https://raw.githubusercontent.com/GASPI-Forum/GASPI-Forum.github.io/master/standards/GASPI-17.1.pdf, [online; accessed 28-May-2024]
3. Hilbrich, T., Schulz, M., de Supinski, B.R., Müller, M.S.: MUST: A scalable approach to runtime error detection in MPI programs. In: Tools for High Performance Computing 2009, pp. 53–66, Springer (2010), https://doi.org/10.1007/978-3-642-11261-4_5
4. Hück, A., Jammer, T., Jenke, J., Bischof, C.: Investigating the Real-World Applicability of MPI Correctness Benchmarks. In: Proceedings of the SC '23 Workshops of The International Conference on High Performance Computing, Network, Storage, and Analysis, pp. 230–233, SC-W '23, ACM (2023). https://doi.org/10.1145/3624062.3624091

5. Hück, A., Jammer, T., Protze, J., Bischof, C.: Investigating the Usage of MPI at Argument-Granularity in HPC Codes. In: Proceedings of EuroMPI2023: the 30th European MPI Users' Group Meeting, pp. 1–10, EuroMPI2023, ACM (2023). https://doi.org/10.1145/3615318.3615322
6. Hück, A., Lehr, J.P., Kreutzer, S., Protze, J., Terboven, C., Bischof, C., Müller, M.S.: Compiler-aided type tracking for correctness checking of MPI applications. In: IEEE/ACM 2nd Intl. Workshop on Software Correctness for HPC Applications (Correctness), pp. 51–58 (2018), https://doi.org/10.1109/Correctness.2018.00011
7. Intel: Intel Trace Analyzer and Collector. https://software.intel.com/content/www/us/en/develop/tools/oneapi/components/trace-analyzer.html   (2023), [online; accessed 28-May-2024]
8. Laguna, I., Marshall, R., Mohror, K., Ruefenacht, M., Skjellum, A., Sultana, N.: A Large-Scale Study of MPI Usage in Open-Source HPC Applications. In: Proceedings of the International Conference for High Performance Computing, Networking, Storage and Analysis, SC '19, ACM (2019), https://doi.org/10.1145/3295500.3356176
9. Laurent, M., Saillard, E., Quinson, M.: The MPI Bugs Initiative: a Framework for MPI Verification Tools Evaluation. In: IEEE/ACM 5th International Workshop on Software Correctness for HPC Applications (Correctness), pp. 1–9 (2021). https://doi.org/10.1109/Correctness54621.2021.00008
10. Lehr, J.P., Jammer, T., Bischof, C.: MPI-CorrBench: Towards an MPI Correctness Benchmark Suite. In: Proceedings of the 30th International Symposium on High-Performance Parallel and Distributed Computing, pp. 69–80, HPDC'21, ACM (2021). https://doi.org/10.1145/3431379.3460652
11. Lin, P.H., Liao, C.: High-Precision Evaluation of Both Static and Dynamic Tools using DataRaceBench. In: 2021 IEEE/ACM 5th International Workshop on Software Correctness for HPC Applications (Correctness), pp. 1–8 (2021), https://doi.org/10.1109/Correctness54621.2021.00011
12. Luecke, G., Coyle, J., Hoekstra, J., Kraeva, M., Xu, Y., Park, M.Y., Kleiman, E., Weiss, O., Wehe, A., Yahya, M.: The Importance of Run-Time Error Detection. pp. 145–155 (01 2009). https://doi.org/10.1007/978-3-642-11261-4_10
13. Message Passing Interface Forum: MPI: A Message-Passing Interface Standard Version 4.1 (Nov 2023), https://www.mpi-forum.org/docs/mpi-4.1/mpi41-report.pdf, [online; accessed 28-May-2024]
14. OpenSHMEM Committee: OpenSHMEM: Application Programming Interface Version 1.5 (2020), http://openshmem.org/site/sites/default/site_files/OpenSHMEM-1.5.pdf, [online; accessed 28-May-2024]
15. Saillard, E., Carribault, P., Barthou, D.: PARCOACH: Combining static and dynamic validation of MPI collective communications. The International Journal of High Performance Computing Applications 28(4), 425–434 (2014). https://doi.org/10.1145/2488551.2488555
16. Schwitanski, S., Jenke, J., Klotz, S., Müller, M.S.: RMARaceBench: A Microbenchmark Suite to Evaluate Race Detection Tools for RMA Programs. In: Proceedings of the SC '23 Workshops of The International Conference on High Performance Computing, Network, Storage, and Analysis, pp. 205–214, SC-W '23, ACM (2023). https://doi.org/10.1145/3624062.3624087
17. Schwitanski, S., Jenke, J., Tomski, F., Terboven, C., Müller, M.S.: On-the-Fly Data Race Detection for MPI RMA Programs with MUST. In: 2022 IEEE/ACM Sixth International Workshop on Software Correctness for HPC Applications (Correctness), pp. 27–36, IEEE (2022), https://doi.org/10.1109/Correctness56720.2022.00009

18. Vinayagame, R., Saillard, E., Thibault, S., Nguyen, V.M., Sergent, M.: Rethinking Data Race Detection in MPI-RMA Programs. In: Proceedings of the SC'23 Workshops of The International Conference on High Performance Computing, Network, Storage, and Analysis, pp. 196–204 (2023), https://doi.org/10.1145/3624062.3624086
19. Virouleau, P., Saillard, E., Sergent, M., Lemarinier, P.: Highlighting PARCOACH Improvements on MBI. In: Workshops of The International Conference on High Performance Computing, Network, Storage, and Analysis, SC-W 2023 (2023). https://doi.org/10.1145/3624062.3624093

Author Index

C. Blaas-Schenner et al. (Eds.): EuroMPI 2024, LNCS 15267, p. 139, 2025.
https://doi.org/10.1007/978-3-031-73370-3